lit from within

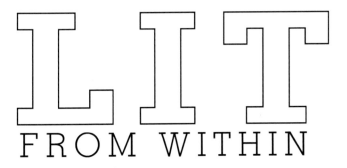

LIT FROM WITHIN

Contemporary Masters on the
Art and Craft of Writing

EDITED BY KEVIN HAWORTH
AND DINTY W. MOORE

Ohio University Press ◆ Athens

Ohio University Press, Athens, Ohio 45701
www.ohioswallow.com
© 2011 by Ohio University Press
All rights reserved

Printed in the United States of America
Ohio University Press books are printed on acid-free paper ⊗ ™

20 19 18 17 16 15 14 13 12 11   5 4 3 2 1

Library of Congress Cataloging-in-Publication Data

Lit from within : contemporary masters on the art and craft of writing / edited
by Kevin Haworth and Dinty W. Moore.
    p. cm.
  Includes bibliographical references.
  ISBN 978-0-8214-1948-9 (pbk. : acid-free paper)
  1. Authorship. I. Haworth, Kevin, 1971– II. Moore, Dinty W., 1955– III. Title.

PN145.L58 2011
808'.02—dc22

                            2010050844

Contents

Acknowledgments

This anthology would never have been possible without the generosity of the authors who have allowed their work to be reprinted here and the countless people over the past twenty-five years who have given support, assistance, attention, and care to Ohio University's Spring Literary Festival.

We'd like to offer specific thanks to those who helped start the Literary Festival in 1986, including College of Arts and Sciences dean F. Donald Eckelmann, English Department chair Duane Schneider, Wayne Dodd, Bob DeMott, Jack Matthews, and Pam Durban. Thanks as well to those who worked to maintain the festival, including Joyce Barlow Dodd, Kate Fox, Bob Kinsley, Jean Cunningham, and numerous faculty members and graduate students whose support and contributions over the years are appreciated though not recorded. More recently, Lydia McDermott, Ami Iannone, and Kiersten Bonifant have been instrumental in keeping the festival ship afloat.

Thanks also to former English Department chair Joe McLaughlin and creative writing faculty Joan Connor, Mark Halliday, Zakes Mda, Jill Rosser, and Darrell Spencer for their support and assistance with this project.

Finally, our thanks to all the staff members at Ohio University Press for their expert care and handling of this project.

Introduction

This book has its origins in the Ohio University Spring Literary Festival, a remarkable yearly gathering of some of the nation's most talented and celebrated writers here in this most rural corner of Ohio. The university brings them here, but the event is not *only* for the campus—for its entire twenty-five-year history, the Lit Fest (as we call it) has been free and welcoming to the public. It is a shining example of public access to art in an unlikely and beautiful setting.

What also distinguishes the Lit Fest is that, from its beginning twenty-five years ago, it has given its writers no theme to follow, no boundaries on what they should read or talk about. An invitation to be a Lit Fest featured writer has required only that, in addition to the usual readings and socializing that characterize such gatherings, all writers must, at some point, stand up for forty-five minutes and talk about writing—the issues of craft that interest them, the elements of the writing life that excite them (or otherwise), the parts of the calling that only one writer can tell another.

Frankly, this has scared some writers off. But those who have agreed to join us here in Athens, Ohio, find themselves speaking, for the benefit of the students, teachers, and others in the audience, to questions like: What makes this work so difficult? What is it possible to do next? And how can I convey to you how much it matters?—those beautiful questions with which all writers grapple.

◆

WHAT WE HAVE tried to do, in this collection, is to reflect the level of the conversation about poetics and the craft of writing that has taken place over the Lit Fest's twenty-five-year history. Our contributors have been generous with their time and their thinking, giving us a number of essays that are being published for the first time here.

We also have chosen to honor the Lit Fest's history by reprinting two essays, one by Charles Baxter and another by Francine Prose, that appear in recent books by those writers. Like several others published here, these essays grew from lectures first delivered at the Spring Literary Festival—continuing the Lit Fest's legacy as an engine for new writing as well as a celebration of writing already completed.

The result is a varied, sometimes funny, and always thoughtful conversation about writing by and for those who are serious about their commitment to this difficult and rewarding art form. The essays gathered here are not limited or organized by genre, but instead are arranged to generate the unexpected collisions of meaning and inspiration that occur when one piece of good writing crosses another. In his essay "Only Collect: Something about the Short Story Collection," Peter Ho Davies celebrates the internal "communities of collections" formed when essays or stories within a book comment on each other in surprising ways. "The assembling of a collection," he writes, whatever its unifying or disunifying factors, is "another step toward how we as writers read ourselves and our work."

◆

AS MOST OF us know, putting a bunch of talented writers together anywhere—a literary festival, a book, a room with an open bar tab—can yield unpredictable and hopefully pleasing results. We see that here. Claire Bateman's essay "Some Questions about Questions," which poses any number of questions a serious writer might consider, has its echoes later in Maggie Nelson's "All That Is the Case: Some Thoughts on Fact in Nonfiction and Documentary Poetry." Nelson takes up the issue of questioning once again, applying the issue particularly to the role of fact in one's work, while directing us finally to Thoreau's clarifying statement for writers: "The question is not what you look at—but how you look & whether you see."

Looking at the self, as both a reader and a writer: this thread, woven by long experience, connects Mary Ruefle's and Stephen Dunn's essays. Ruefle shares a moment that would be devastating to any writer: "When I was forty-five years old, I woke up on an ordinary day, neither sunny nor overcast, in the middle of the year, and I could no longer read." The solution, as it turns out, is reading glasses, but this gives Ruefle the opportunity to examine the multifaceted role reading plays in her life and ours. Dunn, meanwhile, performs an act of reading that many recognize as the most difficult: reading one's own work, twenty years later. He does this carefully, "like an interested stranger," he writes, but like a dedicated parent, too, willing to allow space for the work and himself to grow.

Not all the themes here are retrospective or inward. Many are practical, funny, and rooted in the challenges of the moment. Lee K. Abbott and David Kirby, beyond the obvious fact that their essays both catalogue "Thirteen Things," show that writers are equally obliged to respond to others. Abbott, one of America's acknowledged masters of the short story, explores what he sees as thirteen serious flaws in contemporary short story writing, and challenges today's writers to overcome them. Kirby, one of the greatest current ambassadors for poetry and creativity in general, gives his trademark odd and often hilarious testimony of being a writer—and then tells us, with utter seriousness, how he answers those who would disregard or minimize our work.

Finally, it is worth noting that despite words like "poetry" or "the short story" in the titles of the essays collected here, all of these essays hold valuable advice and thoughtful provocation for writers of any genre—poetry, fiction, or nonfiction. For instance, Carl Dennis's discussion of Louise Glück's poem "Walking at Night" is as much about how a character is built on the page as it is about poetics. (Glück, by the way, is also an Ohio University Spring Literary Festival alum, from our fourth year, 1989.)

◆

AN UNLIKELY CONFLUENCE. That's what any gathering of poets, fiction writers, and nonfiction writers is, after all, when so much of society tells us to find work—and meaning—elsewhere. Our unlikely confluence occurs in Athens, a town founded when, according to one lively account, a wayward explorer crossed the Hocking River while shooting at (but missing) a large buffalo. Settlers from the East Coast soon followed, building cabins of walnut and ash, setting aside funds for the formation of a university outside the original Thirteen Colonies, and naming their town in honor of the city of classical learning. All within the larger context of southeast Ohio, a very rural borderland of the Midwest and Appalachia—a place of economic struggle and natural beauty.

This past quarter century of literary festivity has been both wonderful and memorable. Here's to another twenty-five years.

—*Kevin Haworth and Dinty W. Moore*

lit from within

RON CARLSON was born in Utah and raised in Salt Lake City. His nine works of fiction include his new novel *Five Skies*. Carlson's accolades include Pushcart and O. Henry Prizes and a National Society of Arts and Letters Literature Award. He is also the recipient of a fellowship from the National Endowment for the Arts. Carlson is director of the Graduate MFA Program in Fiction at the University of California at Irvine.

Carlson was a featured writer at the 2007 Ohio University Spring Literary Festival.

The Wrong Answer

RON CARLSON

A FEW YEARS AGO I BEGAN receiving e-mail queries about my story "The Ordinary Son," which had appeared in *The Best American Short Stories*. They were obviously from students, and they all posed the same question: "I was wondering what theme you had in mind when you wrote the story." I answered the first student truly that I do not write for theme. I had begun the story because of a strange job I had when I was seventeen, working maintenance for a motel on the outskirts of Houston, Texas, the summer I made my first fresh blunders at developing a personal life. In the writing, I tried to be true to the events of the summer by describing them closely, because I had learned that if I did that, and assembled a believable inventory, something else would happen in the writing, something I couldn't foresee. The other thing always only happened in the act of writing. In "The Ordinary Son" as soon as I featured the motel and gave it an inventory—somewhat based on memory—the place began to evolve. It began to devolve actually and it became seedier than it was in life, and then I found (in writing) a very old resident of the motel and a scene emerged. I've written dozens of stories this way: paying hard attention and listening as one thing leads to another.

The student wrote back to me and said *this was the wrong answer.*

Her teacher wasn't accepting this answer. Her teacher wanted a composition on theme, and could I please help. I sat up and wondered what to write to this ardent young scholar. I reread her message and, so instructed, I began to help. I wrote to every student as each e-mailed me—a dozen kids (high school students, I judged, though my story seemed a bit graphic for such a group), and in each message I noted that I had this theme in mind or that theme, yes, some rites-of-passage, and some money-can't-bring-you-love or -happiness, and neither can being smart. These things are in the story. I tried hard for these kids, seriously, because the first girl had caught me out. As I read the story again, I saw the possibilities of many themes. These young readers needed suggestions for the meaning of the story, when in fact *as a writer* I was operating on the principle that the story itself is the meaning.

The meaning didn't help me write it; not a bit. But after I'd scrambled with my memory and the inventory of the life I remembered, I had without question crafted many themes. The premise for the way I've been working these many years is still viewed sometimes as the wrong answer.

I know what theme is, and that is: it is a reader's term. It is a term useful to those decoding text. When the work is all done and put in pages somehow, along comes theme. A reader examines the arrangement of the evidence and draws a conclusion or proposes an interpretation of the sometimes tangled persons, places, and happenings in the story. When I taught high school years ago, I had a skeptical sophomore (redundancy acknowledged) who called it DIM, the Deep Inner Meaning. He said it always as if the phrase were framed in golden quotation marks; it was a phrase he used to mock the proceedings. Analyzing literature (essays, poetry, and fiction) is a minor major industry and great sport, and we've all seen the lights go on in students' eyes when the discussion reaches a certain level. We've also seen the lights go out when they turn to the page once again instructed to read foremost for meaning. Do we read foremost for meaning? Don't answer.

I love what Annie Dillard said about theme to writers in her wonderful book on writing, *that if you scratch an event a theme will arise.* I'm an event scratcher. I've always worked from evidence up, not verdict down.

This means that I don't know everything that is going to happen, that I do not know the ending of my stories. I don't parse my evidence before or even as I write a draft. I include absolutely as much as my memory and imagination suggests.

As I noted in my discussion of "The Governor's Ball," I start with a moment. This means that I don't know everything that is going to happen, that I do not know the ending of my stories. I start with a moment. These moments are all sorts of things; I sometimes call them collisions. I have just finished a story which started because as I stood on a friend's porch in Los Angeles one morning after ringing the bell, I looked up the tunnel of jacaranda trees blooming all down her block and with her tall front garden agapanthus swaying around me like seaweed I felt like I was suddenly in a purple town and I heard a sort of Philip Marlowe character saying, "Sometimes this can be a purple town." That's all. What does it mean? I don't know. What will the theme be? Purple? I'll have to write the story. Joining my intuition with those purple trees and a sense of the voice that said ". . . purple town . . ." I would have to write the story. More recently I went into a thrift store I love in Los Angeles hoping to acquire more of the beautiful shirts some guy my size had been donating there for months, and I ran into a young guy who had just bought a gigantic round oak table and he was scratching his head and looking at the little red dolly they'd loaned him to get it home. He lived three blocks away. I stood in that carpeted alcove and I felt the feeling I've had over a hundred times, of being beside myself, of being there and observing myself being there, and as I reached out to steady the beautiful edge of his beautiful table, I knew I was enacting a story idea. Not the story: the event that if I opened it carefully and included everything I knew while I allowed all of the things that would happen to evolve into things that could happen, I would find something out and have a story. What would the theme be? Kindness? The helping hand at the thrift store? No. The story I wrote has a theme, but I couldn't have predicted it until I'd typed the last page.

◆

WE CAN SEE planned themes enacted frequently in films, where many times a writer is not working alone or without the heavy guidance of a focus group or a producer's wallet. Everybody knows that the unearned happy ending is an insult, even to a child. Movie endings are generally fraudulent because of the demands of marketing, so the good folks are going to win. If the good guys don't win, then the film is going to be a small art house film and will be the bittersweet last chapter in the careers of all involved. If there is going to be some question about the good guys winning, then the filmmakers can brighten that with the sound track or the helicopter shot or with an audience within the film clapping madly or throwing their hats and laughing, hugging, smiling. Every audience shot within a film (where we see an ardent group of spectators witnessing the main event) is the heavy hand of a bad author come to instruct us in the use of our emotions, because he or she doesn't trust us to understand the scene. Filmmakers don't trust us very much at all, and are unduly concerned about "how the audience leaves the theater." We know how to leave the theater—up the aisle and out the door. It's enough; it will serve.

If a story depends on its ending, it hasn't done its work. This means, of course, that an unearned mordant ending—a more common feature of literary writing—is an insult as well. Fiction writers don't have sound tracks to trick up their endings, but they have other methods, including all of the various instruments of image and metaphor. An example would be a rainbow; rainbows are sound track and always a bright unmistakable signal that the writer has failed. Rainbows, light bending through prismatic water vapor are 100 percent symbolic in stories. Moonlight or rain on the last two pages means the writer has failed. Starlight: failure. Anything glowing: failure. Distant music (a radio down the block, etc.): failure. Evening falling (evening doing anything): failure. Darkness modified by any adjective: failure. A smile in the last paragraph: failure. Appearance of a bird on the last page: failure. A group of people throwing their hats and hugging: failure. There are so many ways to attempt to cheat the reader and thereby fail. *Cheryl looked at me, her eyes glistening, and I could see the starlight reflected there, and she walked away in the rain.* Cheryl may walk away. I sort of hope she doesn't. But if she walks away, she's going to have to do it without glistening and without the aid of the starlight or the rain. It's a good writer who can have Cheryl walk away without the night or the rain. It's a great writer—or one with real ambition—who can have her hesitate and extend the ambiguity.

Of course, what I am saying with such pretty axioms is that every story must earn its ending, dark or light. (Rain is rain and you can have it if it is precipitation and not meteorological sound track.) Stories earn their endings via evidence. The evidence, in my case, isn't arranged and selected beforehand and delivered to the site. It can only be found in the pure act of writing. One thing leads to another in a world a writer discovers. To plan the evidence is exactly the same as tampering with the scene of a crime. This is oversimplified, and I don't exactly mean crime. Wherever a story goes it must earn its belief, and the person who must believe it is the writer. If I do that there is a chance the readers will come along later, and they have shown themselves to be relentless about finding my theme.

But wait, Dear Professor. When I looked again at my story "The Ordinary Son" I saw that it ended in the rain. It's raining in Houston! The two young geniuses are standing in the light rain and the narrator, knowing they are geniuses, says, "I counted on their being able to find a way out of it."

I bit my lip for a second and then thought: that's okay. It's raining. I'm keeping it.

I answered one of the last e-mails I received about my story "The Ordinary Son" by illuminating yet another possible theme, this time citing the genius father's drafting table that blocks the entrance of their house and creates the theme of work, and then I told the student that his teacher owed me a double milkshake by now for helping her class with its papers. The student wrote back. He was in Montreal, and the story— along with the questions about theme—was on the provincial year-end exams. He said he was going to sneak a copy from the room the next day and copy it in the library for me. As I typed my reply, hoping to avoid an international incident, I had that little thrill of recognition again: a story idea. Some kid raises his hand in Canada and asks to go to the washroom. Inside his jacket are the secret documents.

ROBIN HEMLEY has published seven books, including *Do-Over! In which a forty-eight-year-old father of three returns to kindergarten, summer camp, the prom, and other embarrassments.* His stories and essays have appeared in the *New York Times, New York Magazine, Chicago Tribune,* and many literary magazines and anthologies. Hemley received his MFA from the Iowa Writers Workshop; he currently directs the Nonfiction Writing Program at the University of Iowa and lives in Iowa City, Iowa.

Hemley was a featured writer at the 2010 Ohio University Spring Literary Festival.

Confessions of a Navel Gazer

(In which a whiny, self-promoting, and narcissistic writer of memoir rants unimaginatively about his dreary little scribblings)

ROBIN HEMLEY

WHEN I WAS IN GRADUATE school in the 1980s my friends and I used to classify writers into two types: windows and mirrors. The mirrors were the poets, writers of reflection and meditation. The fiction writers were the windows, writers who looked out on the wide world and wrote about what they saw. Of course, the analogy was simplistic—fiction writers can be reflective and poets can write about the world outside themselves, but that was the basic dichotomy as we understood it. My grad school even broke into softball teams: the Windows versus the Mirrors.

But on which team did the poor nonfiction writers play, the memoirists in particular? They could play on neither team. They weren't even the water carriers, the bat boys and girls. That's because memoirists as we know them today didn't exist.

In fact, it was considered the height of arrogance and pomposity to suggest writing your *memwahs* (preferably said with a French accent) if you were not a famous general, actor, or politician. There were no schools for memoirists, no classes, no books on how to write a memoir. The lives of ordinary people as such were considered, well, ordinary. Who wanted to read about ordinariness? A well-known movie at the time, called *Ordinary People,* revealed shockingly that ordinary people have feelings and secrets and tragedies, too. Who would have thought?! Betraying a cultural suspicion that this could not truly be the case, Bette Davis, in reading the nominees for Best Picture that year at the Oscars, renamed the film, "Ordinary Movie." Ordinary or not, this film from 1980 took away four Oscars, including Best Picture, Best Director (Robert Redford), Best Actor (Timothy Hutton), and Best Adapted Screenplay. And no wonder. The most persistent and sacred of lies is that any family is perfect, and yet families go to great lengths to preserve this myth. That's essentially what this film was about—in an affluent family, one of the sons dies in an accident and the family, especially the parents, pretends it never happened. But the son, Timothy Hutton, completely messed up as a result of his family's dysfunction (the term was not common parlance back then), sees a psychiatrist, Judd Hirsch, who heals Timothy Hutton by urging him to speak the truth, thus allowing him to win an Oscar. Okay, not quite as simple as that. Perhaps I'm betraying *my* cynical Bette Davis side.

As it turns out, a lot of people not only wanted to watch a movie about the large tragedies of small lives, but to read about them, too. And oddly, not as fiction. In the past, what we might call a memoir now was typically the writer of fiction's first novel, what's known as a *roman à clef* (this, preferably said in a British accent), or a thinly veiled autobiographical novel. In my parents' day, it was great literary sport to read a novel and try to figure out who the writer was *really* writing about. When Thomas Wolfe wrote his famous novel, *Look Homeward Angel,* he literally couldn't go home again to his hometown of Asheville, North Carolina. Everyone knew exactly whom he was referring to and what he was writing about and they were hopping mad. About five years after publication of the novel, when Wolfe was a world-famous novelist, the only people who remained angry in Asheville were the people he *hadn't* written about.

♦

WITH THE RISE of the memoir over the last thirty years, writers by the scores have written about their hometowns and much more. Now there *are* courses for writers of memoir to take and books to read on the subject. If we ever thought before that the people around us were ordinary, we don't think so any longer. In fact, we know that if anything, nearly everyone can tell you a story of their family brimming with secrets and skeleton-packed closets.

But for every memoir-equivalent of an emotive Not-a-dry-eye-in-the-house Oscar-winning performance, there's a Bette Davis standing up there grumbling that she's been lowered to this, that the arts have been lowered to celebrating the meaningless little traumas of suburbanites. Usually, it's a poet or a fiction writer, sadly sometimes a nonfiction writer, who (and this is very important) wouldn't stoop to writing a memoir, and joins the literary grousing. "Ordinary memoir!"

And they have a point.

To me, the film *Ordinary People* marks a watershed in our cultural fascination and phobia with telling our dirty little secrets. I'm not claiming that the film was responsible for the steady climb in memoirs written by ordinary people, starting around that time, but that the film tapped into a cultural shift that's both positive and negative in its literary ramifications. Around this time, I started noticing an unsophisticated suspicion of anything not labeled as "fact." "I only read true stories," strangers have more than once told me, betraying a certain literal-mindedness in the American psyche that's frightening. This suspicion of anything that isn't "factual" is its literary manifestation. In a way we have become a nation of literary fundamentalists—we care about something only if we think it really truly happened. We watch TV only if it really happened. American fiction for many years had been moving steadily toward realism, entrenching it within the academy as THE only proper form of fiction, but once ordinary people started writing memoir, the idea of realism jumped the tracks. Why read fiction when nonfiction did realism better? It seemed the difference between looking out of a dirty train window and a clean one.

This reminds me in some ways of what happened to the painting world in the nineteenth century when photography was introduced. As soon as one could point a machine at a table and effortlessly create a mass-produced image that was far more accurate than a painting, the need for paintings to represent the empirical world mostly vanished, and what resulted was a greater move toward abstraction in painting, though of course photography didn't restrict itself to the literal image for long either. But the split between fiction and nonfiction seems much more intractable. It's been cast in the popular imagination as the difference between the real and unreal, between truth and lies. The loser in all this has been the Imagination. What we've seen over the past thirty years in the American readership is a steady erosion of the value of imaginative writing, in everything that is nonliteral. As one friend of mine put it recently, "Short stories are the new poetry and novels are the new short story." When Flannery O'Connor spoke nearly fifty years ago at the University of Chicago about the literal, she spoke of it this way: "A short story writer is literal in the way a child's drawing is literal. The child does not aim to distort, but as his gaze is direct, he records the lines that create motion. For the serious writer, it is the lines that create spiritual motion that interest him."

This is no less true today, or should be no less true. The writer's gaze should be direct and should not aim to slavishly record reality but to x-ray it, to see its inner workings.

I wonder now if I were back in graduate school, where we would place memoirists in the window/mirror debate. I'd venture that most memoirists would consider themselves "mirrors" (if they chose to play this mirror/window game at all!). Certainly, memoirs most often deal with reflection, with looking back upon an event or a time in one's life, often childhood, when the world pitched its mysteries, conflagrations, and confabulations at the poor child, to sort out later. Much later. Memoirs are often about the "sorting out," or as the writer Bernard Cooper elegantly states, "A good memoir filters a life through resonant narrative, and in doing so must achieve a balance between language and candor. It was not the subject matter of my memoirs that I hoped would be startling, but rather language's capacity to name what was once nameless, to define what had once been vague and chaotic. The chief privilege of writing a memoir was the opportunity to go back and make sense of events that left me dumbstruck, mired in confusion, unarmed with the luminous power of words." That last phrase is the key here: "the luminous power of words."

Critics of memoirs often bandy about the term "navel gazers" when they want to suggest the whiny-ness and self-indulgence of memoirists. A great way to get applause at a writer's conference or among an audience of journalists is to suggest that writers should go out and study the secret life of rocks or the mating habits of the narwhal or the illegitimate children of the popes: anything but the self, anything but navel-gazing.

I wonder though—aren't poets navel gazers? Aren't fiction writers navel gazers? Isn't navel-gazing really another, more pejorative term for "interiority"? As a fiction writer, non-fiction writer, and occasional poet, the son of a poet and a short story writer, I see essentially no difference between the amount of navel-gazing necessary in any artistic endeavor. The autobiographical poem is acceptable in polite society, as is the autobiographical novel or short story, but the memoir is crass and sensational because . . . because . . . I guess you've lost me here.

Interiority is not a major concern of straight-ahead non-fiction as it is of the poet, the fiction writer, the memoirist, and the personal essayist. Read Michael Pollan's *Omnivore's Dilemma,* and you might be moved to buy local or grow your own food. Read Jared Diamond's *Guns, Germs, and Steel,* and you'll have a better understanding of the complex power dynamics that have shaped the worlds' civilizations. Read Bill Bryson's *In a Sunburned Country,* and you'll have an entertaining look at all the many things that can kill you if you visit Australia. I recommend them all—to various degrees, you'll be entertained, informed, and awed. But they most likely won't work on you the way a poem, short story, or memoir will.

The kind of navel-gazing that the memoirist, the poet, and the fiction writer are all interested in reveals the interior truths of small lives. This should be no less important than large truths of civilizations. I don't know any other way to put it than I wonder how we can hope to understand the world at large in any meaningful way if we don't confront the secrets we carry inside. The human heart in conflict with itself, as Faulkner wrote.

One thing we have to stress repeatedly is that yes, there ARE bad memoirs. There ARE memoirs that are sensational. There ARE memoirs that are poorly written. There ARE memoirists who are self-indulgent, truculent, mean-spirited, bad-smelling, finicky eaters, liars, narcissists, cheaters at board games, and criminally insane. We must stress this because there are NO bad poems, NO bad short stories, NO bad pieces of reportage, NO journalists or straight-ahead nonfiction writers who have ever made up a fact, told a lie, written something sensational, exploited anyone, or written something knowingly skewed to prove a point. There are NO narcissistic poets and NO narcissistic fiction writers. Not a navel gazed or even grazed.

So, on behalf of all memoirists, let me say this: We are sorry. Deeply sorry we have been so self-indulgent and bad. We promise we will not be bad again (Note to self: After uttering this line, slap your hand hard).

There are plenty of fiction writers and poets who would not put memoirists in the same category as themselves: Writers of the Imagination (Note to self: In public presentation, Photoshop pictures of O'Connor, Rushdie, Alice Munro, and Aleksandar Hemon on horseback, looking out from a butte as a storm gathers in the distance), and it's understandable why they might refuse memoirists entry into the vaunted Halls of Literature. Aleksandar Hemon might be typical of such sentiment in an interview in the *Missouri Review*. Recalling how callers to a radio talk show spoke about one of the characters in his novel as though that character actually existed, he says, "[A] large number of people that day believed, I mean, they believed and they said Thank you for discovering this amazing character [and] . . . I started thinking, *What if there's someone who knows more about him than me?* That is, What if he is sort of actualized now? What if someone calls in and says, 'You are lying; he didn't really do that.' Not 'You're lying; he doesn't really exist,' but 'You are lying; he was not buried in Finland; he was buried somewhere else.' . . . I had the sense of the presence of this man, who was blatantly made up. . . . No memoir can compare to that. Because I already exist, if I write my memoir that just confirms what already exists. I made up Rora and all that. I made it up, to some extent. That's the exciting part."

At this point in the interview, Hemon gets so jazzed by his imaginative powers that he says he's going to go home to write, and the interview ends. We, of course, sit in awe somewhere along the trail, eating his literary dust.

But something he says gives me a sliver of hope, his seeming caveat, "I made it up, *to some extent,*" because this small phrase, easily overlooked, would suggest a grudging or passing acknowledgment of what I firmly believe, that all good writing is a combustible mix of experience and imagination. As a writer of both fiction and nonfiction, I know that writing fiction can often take as much research in the "real world" as nonfiction, and that much fiction contains observed experience if not autobiography. Much nonfiction is recreated experience—recreating a scene or conversation from thirty years earlier takes no less imagination than the fiction writer creating a dialogue, though I will concede Hemon one point. The invention of a believable fictional character readers feel passionately about as though he existed gives fiction writers some bragging rights. It's a feat of the imagination. But I would venture that to create *any* character whom the reader feels passionately about, whether he or she lived or not, should give *any* writer bragging rights. If that character happens to be me, or a version of me, I'm not sure that makes a case for some kind of genre deficiency or evidence of a weak imagination. Contrary to Hemon's statement, the memoirist doesn't simply paste himself into a book and say, "Look at me! There I am in all my navel-gazing glory!" To anyone who thinks it's easy, I'd say the same thing that I say to anyone who thinks writing a piece of fiction is easy, "Go ahead and write a memoir. See how easy it is. See how unimaginative it is."

The writer of nonfiction might be starting with events that really happened, but recreating them is an imaginative feat. Ordering them is an imaginative feat. Making sense of them is an imaginative feat.

So on the one hand memoirists take some heat from fiction writers for not being imaginative enough and on the other we take heat for not being literal enough. I'm not talking about James Frey or other mostly invented memoirs, but about the people who read my book or another memoir and want to know whether I'm healed.

This question always terrifies me. I didn't know I needed to be healed, but leaving that aside for the moment, it's still a question that stymies me. "After writing _____, did you feel healed?"

It's an innocent enough question, and I'm not trying to be critical of the journalists and ordinary people (those pesky ordinary people!) who ask it repeatedly, but the problem is that there's no simple answer. I suppose it depends what your intention is for writing—to me, healing suggests something permanent. Something gets better. But in my experience, there's no permanence in life. You write something and perhaps it moves a reader and moves you as well. But does it heal you? There's a literal-mindedness to the question that plays into the hands of those who would call memoirists "navel gazers."

The question makes me want to question the questioner: MUST I be healed? Is that a requirement? If I haven't been healed, does that mean I've failed to write a good book? I'm afraid that some people (readers, writers, editors, talk show hosts, filmmakers, softball players) might answer, We EXPECT redemption. We EXPECT results! We expect your own little Judd Hirsch to coax your awful secrets out of you and at the very least, begin the healing process . . .

But is this what literature does? Shouldn't literature leave healing to the therapists? I never read, say, Flannery O'Connor's classic short story "A Good Man Is Hard to Find" to be healed or redeemed. And by the way, her story is about ordinary people, too, a family from Atlanta who take a drive and wind up murdered by an insane escaped convict by the name of the Misfit. Everyone in the family other than the cat, Pitty Sing, dies. And yet as those who have read the story know, it's precisely about redemption. Okay, it's elegant redemption. It's not Spill-your-guts-to-Judd-Hirsch-and-win-an-Oscar redemption. Although there is literal gut-spilling in the deaths of O'Connor's ordinary people, you never see it. It happens offstage in the woods of a lonely country road, to be precise, and you must use your imagination to picture the results of that faraway gunshot. Famously, the Misfit, after shooting the selfish grandmother in the story, remarks, "She would of been a good woman if it had been someone there to shoot her every minute of her life." She's redeemed in the story in a moment of grace (of the Christian Variety) in which she loses her selfishness for presumably the only time in her life. But was Flannery O'Connor healed by writing the story?

As a memoir writer, I'm the grandmother, the Misfit, and Flannery O'Connor all rolled into one. I'm writing about myself, yes, but writing about a younger self most often, trying to make sense of my selfishness, my craziness, and heartlessness armed as Bernard Cooper states with "the luminous power of words." When someone asks if I'm healed I want to answer, "I'd be healed if I wrote a memoir every minute of my life." In my experience, healing is as fleeting as "goodness."

But I don't blame someone for wanting to know if I've been healed or not. I suppose I should take it as a compliment that anyone would care, but writers of memoir are skilled at writing about themselves as characters. No one is skilled enough to capture him or herself completely on the page in all of his multifaceted and sometimes duplicitous glory. The person on the page is a representation, like a character in a story. The difference of course is that Holden Caulfield and Scout don't exist while I do. You wouldn't ask Scout if she's healed or Holden if he's healed, but how many countless people have wished they could meet Holden or Scout in the flesh? As for, say, Frank McCourt, we think we know the real Frank McCourt, but we don't. We know a version of him that he put in his several books. The two Frank McCourts are related but not the same. I heard him give a lecture once at a conference and he was a charming raconteur, but did I feel I knew him afterwards? No. That's also why, when someone asks me how I feel about this celebrity's divorce or that celebrity's affair, I invariably answer something along the lines of, "I don't know _____. I've never met _____. I wouldn't presume to comment on _____'s affair with _____ though I did once spot _____ from afar in Santa Monica and I said to my wife, 'I think _____ looks pretty good now that she's stopped torturing herself over _____.'"

In my perfect literary world, the distinctions to make finally wouldn't be between Windows and Mirrors, or even genre distinctions, but between the Literal and Imaginative. To me, that's all that matters. Either you are literal-minded or you're not. The altar at which I worship is unabashedly dedicated to the ambiguities of artistic expression, regardless of genre. We all have interior lives worth exploring, though not all of us do. As Emerson wrote, "To believe what is true for you in your private heart is true for all men—that is genius. Speak your latent conviction, and it shall be the universal sense." So, for me, it might ultimately make things simpler if at Barnes and Noble there was a Literal Section and an Imaginative Section. You'd most likely find me (if you knew me) pacing the Imaginative Section, trying to settle on something remarkable to read.

FRANCINE PROSE is the author of many bestselling books of fiction, including *A Changed Man* and *Blue Angel,* which was a finalist for the National Book Award, and the nonfiction *New York Times* bestseller *Reading Like a Writer.* Her novel *Household Saints* was adapted for a movie by Nancy Savoca. Another novel, *The Glorious Ones,* has been adapted into a musical of the same name by Lynn Ahrens and Stephen Flaherty, which ran at the Mitzi E. Newhouse Theatre at Lincoln Center in New York City in the fall of 2007. Her latest book, *Anne Frank: The Book, The Life, The Afterlife,* was published in 2009. She is a former president of PEN American Center. She lives in New York City.

Prose was a featured writer at the 2006 Ohio University Spring Literary Festival.

Gesture

FRANCINE PROSE

CHANNEL SURFING ONE NIGHT, I watched the last twenty minutes of a made-for-TV movie about a small-town girl who gets pregnant and gives up her baby and leaves her boyfriend. Decades later she is reunited with the baby's father when the baby (a grown man, minister, about to become a father himself) locates his parents and brings them together. At the end of the film, the long-separated teen parents (now in late middle age) are married by their son, the reverend, after a brief scene in which the groom gets out of the car and goes to pick up his bride.

The groom straightens his tie, pats down his hair, paces, checks his reflection in the car mirror, straightens his tie, smoothes his hair, fixes his tie again. It's not as if a man in this situation might *not* straighten his tie and smooth his hair, but the familiarity of the gestures, amplified by repetition, shredded the already-fragile veil of illusion surrounding this tender scene.

Perhaps I should say that my definition of gesture includes small physical actions, often unconscious or semi-reflective, including what is called body language and excluding larger, more definite or momentous actions. I would not call picking up a gun and shooting someone a gesture. On the other hand, language—that is, word choice—can function as a gesture: the way certain married people refer to their spouses as *him* or *her* is sort of a gesture communicating possession, intimacy, pride, annoyance, tolerance, or some combination of the above.

Mediocre writing abounds with physical clichés and stock gestures. Opening a mass-market thriller at random, I read: "Clenching her fists so hard she can feel her nails digging into the palms of her hands she forces herself to walk over to him. . . . She snuggled closer to Larry as she felt his arms tighten around her and his sweet breath warm the back of her neck. . . . She adjusted her cap as she crunched down the gravel driveway. . . . Tom bit his lip." All of these are perfectly acceptable English sentences describing common gestures, but they feel generic. They are not descriptions of an individual's very particular response to a particular event, but rather a shorthand for common psychic states. He bit his lip, she clenched her fists—our characters are nervous. The cap-adjuster is wary and determined, the couple intimate, and so forth.

Writers cover pages with familiar reactions (her heart pounded, he wrung his hands) to familiar situations. But unless what the character does is unexpected or unusual, or truly important to the narrative, the reader will assume that response without having to be told. On hearing that his business partner has just committed a murder, a man might be quite upset, and we can intuit that without needing to hear about the speed of his heartbeat or the dampness of his palms. On the other hand, if he's glad his partner has been caught, or if he himself is the murderer, and he smiles . . . well, that's a different story.

Too often, gestures are used as markers, to create beats and pauses in a conversation that, we fear, may rush by too quickly without them.

> "Hello," she said, reaching for a cigarette.
> "Hello," he replied.
> "How are you?" She lit her cigarette.
> "Fine." He poured two glasses of wine.

One might ask why we need to linger over this conversation, why we can't just be permitted to hurry through it, though I suppose the gestures (cigarette, wine) are meant to communicate a certain portentousness. Or something. In any case, the catalogue of gestures will not be improved much if we learn that her hand shook as she lit her cigarette, but it might be given a bit of an edge if we learn that he poured one glass of wine, and then remembered and poured two, or that he poured his own glass—or her glass—much fuller than the other.

If a character's going to light a cigarette, or almost light a cigarette, it should *mean* something as it does in this scene from ZZ Packer's story "Drinking Coffee Elsewhere." A tense interview with a college student makes a psychiatrist nervous enough to reach for a smoke, and the question of whether he can light up or not leads to an exchange in which the student briefly takes control, and the doctor just as quickly grabs it back.

> *"Tell me about your parents."*
> *I wondered what he already had on file. The folder was thick, though I hadn't said a thing of significance since Day One.*
> *"My father was a dick and my mother seemed to like him."*
> *He patted his pockets for his cigarettes. "That's some heavy stuff," he said. "How do you feel about Dad?" The man couldn't say the word "father." "Is Dad someone you see often?"*
> *"I hate my father almost as much as I hate the word 'Dad.'"*
> *He started tapping his cigarette.*
> *"You can't smoke in here."*
> *"That's right," he said, and slipped the cigarette back into the packet. He smiled, widening his eyes brightly. "Don't ever start."*

Much about the relationship between age and youth, social position and suspicion is revealed by the anxious hesitation of the customers in Junot Diaz's story "Edison, New Jersey," which concerns some boys who work delivering card and pool tables:

> *Sometimes the customer has to jet to the store for cat food or a newspaper while we're in the middle of a job. I'm sure you'll be all right, they say. They never sound too sure. Of course, I say. Just show us where the silver's at. The customers ha-ha and we ha-ha and then they agonize over leaving, linger by the front door, trying to memorize everything they own, as if they don't know where to find us, who we work for.*

One could say that everything that happens in Philip Roth's *Goodbye, Columbus* can be predicted, more or less accurately, from the succession of swift gestures that begins the novel. Much of what we need to know about the lovers at the book's center is succinctly telegraphed by the entitled, sexually confident insouciance with which the privileged Brenda Patimkin asks the novel's narrator—a stranger who is merely a day guest at her country club—to hold her glasses before she dives into the pool, and then, knowing he is watching, adjusts her bathing suit:

> *The first time I saw Brenda she asked me to hold her glasses. Then she stepped out to the edge of the diving board and looked foggily into the pool; it could have been drained, myopic Brenda would never have known it. She dove beautifully, and a moment later she was swimming back to the side of the pool, her head of short-clipped auburn hair held up, straight ahead of her, as though it were a rose on a long stem. She glided to the edge and then was beside me. "Thank you," she said, her eyes watery though not from the water. She extended a hand for her glasses but did not put them on until she turned and headed away. I watched her move off. Her hands suddenly appeared behind her. She caught the bottom of her suit between thumb and index finger and flicked what flesh had been showing back where it belonged. My blood jumped.*

A wealth of very different information comes to us through gesture in a scene that Raymond Chandler describes, one that took place in the 1940s, when men more often wore hats: A man and his wife are riding up in the elevator. The door opens. A pretty young woman gets on. The man takes off his hat. And observe how much is conveyed by the moment in Tolstoy's *Resurrection* when a society woman, conscious that she is aging and desperate to appear young, keeps turning from her festive lunch to eye the window through which a beam of unflattering sunlight has begun to shine.

Properly used gestures—plausible, in no way stagy or extreme, yet unique and specific—are like windows opening to let us see a person's soul, his or her secret desires, fears, or obsessions, the precise relations between that person and the self, between the self and the world, as well as (in the Chandler story) the complicated emotional, social, and historical male-female choreography that is instantly comprehensible, even in these hatless times.

Though we may associate Henry James with the complex, long-winded sentence, one of the crucial plot turns in *The Portrait of a Lady* occurs without any heed for words. It happens during the famous scene in which Isabel Archer walks into her drawing room to find her husband, Gilbert Osmond, talking to Madame Merle. Their postures and gestures make Isabel see that the "friendship" between them has been more intimate than she'd imagined. And we too understand exactly what is going on even if we don't live in an era in which, if a gentleman is lounging while a woman stands, the woman is either his mother, his sister, his wife, or in the case of Madame Merle, his mistress and the mother of his child.

> *Madame Merle was there in her bonnet, and Gilbert Osmond was talking to her; for a minute they were unaware she had come in. Isabel had often seen that before, certainly; but what she had not seen, or at least had not noticed, was that their colloquy had for the moment converted itself into a sort of familiar silence, from which she instantly perceived that her entrance would startle them. Madame Merle was standing on the rug, a little way from the fire; Osmond was in a deep chair, leaning back and looking at her. Her head was erect, as usual, but her eyes were bent on his. What struck Isabel first was that he was sitting while Madame Merle stood; there was an anomaly in this that arrested her. Then she perceived that they had arrived at a desultory pause in their exchange of ideas and were musing, face to face, with the freedom of old friends who sometimes exchange ideas without uttering them. There was nothing to shock in this; they were old friends in fact. But the thing made an image, lasting only a moment, like a sudden flicker of light. Their relative positions, their absorbed mutual gaze, struck her as something detected. But it was all over by the time she had fairly seen it. Madame Merle had seen her and had welcomed her without moving; her husband, on the other hand, had instantly jumped up.*

Even in a surreal story, such as Kafka's "The Judgment," gesture can be used to anchor the fiction in a recognizable human context. As Georg Bendemann's father keeps shrinking and growing, gaining and losing personal power, his gestures (the playing with the watch-chain, the throwing off of the bedclothes) keep us apprised of his terrifyingly enlarged or diminished condition, even as Georg's gestures are those of a man attempting to remain calm and reasonable and to make the best of an extremely bizarre situation:

> He carried his father in his arms to the bed. During his few steps toward it he noticed with a terrible sensation that his father, as he lay against his breast, was playing with his watch-chain. He could not put him down on the bed straightaway, so firmly did he cling to his watch-chain.
>
> But no sooner was he in bed when all seemed well. He covered himself up and drew the blanket extra high over his shoulders. He looked up at Georg with a not unfriendly eye.
>
> "There you are, you're beginning to remember it now, aren't you?" Georg asked, nodding at him encouragingly.
>
> "Am I well covered up now?" asked his father, as if he couldn't quite see whether his feet were properly tucked in.
>
> "So you're feeling quite snug in bed already," said Georg, and arranged the bedclothes more firmly around him.
>
> "Am I well covered up?" he asked once more, and seemed to await the answer with special interest.
>
> "Don't worry, you're well covered up."
>
> "No!" shouted his father, and, sending the answer resounding against the question, flung back the blanket with such force that for an instant it unfurled flat in the air, and he stood up erect on the bed. He steadied himself gently with one hand against the ceiling. "You wanted to cover me up, I know that, you young scoundrel, but I'm not covered up yet."

Among the most touching, compressed, and communicative gestures in all of literature occurs in Chekhov's "The Bishop." Our hero, the bishop, is dying. Despite his high position in the church, despite his servants and his ecclesiastical entourage, he is dying alone, cut off from his family, from his own humble origins, and especially from his mother who—quite by accident—comes to visit him, after a long separation. In this scene, the bishop is having lunch with his mother and her granddaughter, the bishop's eight-year-old niece, Katya. One gesture—the business with the drinking glasses—conveys the mother's social unease, her bewilderment in the presence of this important, successful stranger, her son, and a capsule of history of the bishop's upward mobility.

He could see she was constrained as though she were uncertain whether to address him formally or familiarly, to laugh or not, and that she felt herself more a deacon's widow than his mother. And Katya gazed without blinking at her uncle, his holiness, as though trying to discover what sort of person he was. Her hair sprang up from under the comb and the velvet ribbon stood out like a halo; she had a turned up nose and sly eyes. The child had broken a glass before sitting down for dinner, and now her grandmother as she talked moved away from Katya first a wine glass and then a tumbler. The bishop listened to his mother and remembered how many, many years ago she used to take him and his brothers and sisters to relations whom she considered rich.

Later, when the bishop is lying ill in bed, he hears from an adjoining room the sound of crockery breaking as Katya drops a cup or saucer, an action that makes us wonder if what we have observed is not only the grandmother's nervousness but the granddaughter's, as well. Eventually, the little girl summons all her courage and asks the bishop for some money because the family is very poor. So perhaps her clumsiness may not be simply a character trait, or even a result of her youth, but rather a situational response to her own anxiety about how to approach her distinguished uncle on this delicate matter.

Yet another famous literary gesture concludes the opening scene of Joyce's "The Dead"—the exquisitely uncomfortable exchange between the self-important Gabriel Conroy, arriving at his elderly aunt's house for their annual Christmas party, and the aunt's servant, Lily.

—Tell me, Lily, he said in a friendly tone, do you still go to school?

> —O, no, sir, she answered. I'm done schooling this year and more.
>
> —O, then, said Gabriel gaily, I suppose we'll be going to your wedding one of these fine days with your young man, eh?
>
> The girl glanced back at him over her shoulder and said with great bitterness:
>
> —The men that is now is only all palaver and what they can get out of you.
>
> Gabriel coloured as if he felt he had made a mistake and, without looking at her, kicked off his galoshes and flicked actively with his muffler at his patent-leather shoes . . .
>
> When he had flicked luster into his shoes he stood up and pulled his waistcoat down more tightly on his plump body. Then he took a coin rapidly from his pocket.
>
> —O Lily, he said, thrusting it into her hands, it's Christmas-time, isn't it? Just . . . here's a little. . . .
>
> He walked rapidly towards the door.
>
> —O no, sir! cried the girl, following him. Really, sir, I wouldn't take it.
>
> —Christmas-time! Christmas-time! said Gabriel, almost trotting to the stairs and waving his hand to her in deprecation.
>
> The girl, seeing that he had gained the stairs, called out after him:
>
> —Well, thank you, sir.

Gabriel's clumsily giving Lily the coin is the culmination of their awkward exchange; it undermines the inappropriate sexual suggestiveness of his half-flirtatious inquiry about the young man, his patronizing attitude, their mutual awareness of class difference, power, gender, etc. And it prepares us for what we will see Gabriel do throughout the story; take the wrong tone, misinterpret, draw the incorrect conclusions. The smaller gestures that punctuate Gabriel's talk with Lily—his polishing his shoes and straightening his waistcoat—are not the stock tics frequently used (as in the TV movie) as shorthand for anxiety but rather the natural reflexes of a man whose principal struggle is against the fragility of his own vanity, a man who can hardly see the world beyond his defensive self-regard. It's also a sublimely accurate presentation of the way that, following some petty embarrassment or after committing some faux pas, we may find ourselves hurrying to the mirror to gaze at the person who could have done such a thing and, if possible, ever so slightly to improve the face that this person presents to the world.

Gabriel reflects (as we all do) on the larger implications of his small social mistake and attempts to repair his pride with the comforts of his own importance:

> He waited outside the drawing-room door until the waltz should finish. . . . He was still discomposed by the girl's bitter and sudden retort. It had cast a gloom over him which he tried to dispel by arranging his cuffs and the bows of his tie. Then he took from his waistcoat pocket a little paper and glanced at the headings he had made for his speech. He was undecided about the lines from Robert Browning, for he feared they would be above the heads of his hearers. . . . The indelicate clacking of the men's heels and the shuffling of their soles reminded him that their grade of culture differed from his.

The economy with which gesture reveals the prickly consciousness of social class reminds me of a story I heard about a German theater troupe rehearsing a scene in which a boss was supposed to hand a document to a worker in the plant. The actor playing the worker kept saying that he couldn't get the scene right, that something felt incorrect about the way that the worker was taking the document from his boss. At which point the director—Bertolt Brecht, in the version I heard—called in the theater's cleaning woman. Very politely, he said that they were having a problem. Could she help them and hold their document for a moment? The cleaning woman wiped her hands on her apron and only then reached for the paper, thus demonstrating for the actor what had been missing and what was required.

Unlike dialogue, gesture can delineate character when there is only one character in the room. Charles Baxter's "The Cures for Love" begins with a gesture that illuminates its protagonist's domestic and romantic situation:

> On the day he left her for good, she put on one of his caps. It fit snugly over her light brown hair. The cap had the

manufacturer's name of his pickup truck embossed above the visor
in gold letters. She wore the cap backward, the way he once had,
while she cooked dinner. Then she kept it on in her bath that
evening. When she leaned back in the tub, the visor hitting the
tiles, she could smell his sweat from the inside of his headband,
even over the smell of the soap. His sweat had always smelled like
freshly-broiled whitefish.

And Katherine Mansfield's "The Fly" turns on a single gesture performed in solitude, or at least with no other humans present, an action that at first seems obvious in its meaning and import but that grows more complex the longer we think about it. The protagonist, identified only as "the boss," is visited by a friend who happens to mention the grave of the boss's son, killed six years before in the First World War, a death the boss never mentions and tries not to think about. Stricken with anguish, the boss suddenly notices that a fly has fallen into his inkpot:

> *The boss took up a pen, picked the fly out of the ink, and shook it*
> *on to a piece of blotting-paper. For a fraction of a second it lay still*
> *on the dark patch that oozed around it. Then the front legs waved,*
> *took hold, and, pulling its small, sodden body up, it began the*
> *immense task of cleaning the ink from its wings. Over and under,*
> *over and under, went a leg along a wing as the stone goes over and*
> *under the scythe. Then there was a pause, while the fly, seeming*
> *to stand on the tips of its toes, tried to expand first one wing and*
> *then the other. It succeeded at last, and sitting down, it began,*
> *like a minute cat, to clean its face. Now one could imagine that*
> *the little front legs rubbed against each other lightly, joyful. The*
> *horrible danger was over; it had escaped; it was ready for life again.*
>
> *But just then the boss had an idea. He plunged his pen back*
> *into the ink, leaned his thick wrist on the blotting-paper, and as*
> *the fly tried its wings down came a great heavy blot. What would*
> *it make of that? What indeed! The little beggar seemed absolutely*
> *cowed, stunned, and afraid to move because of what would happen*
> *next. But then, as if painfully, it dragged itself forward. The front*
> *legs waved, caught hold, and, more slowly this time, the task*
> *began from the beginning.*

He's a plucky little devil, thought the boss, and he felt a real admiration for the fly's courage. That was the way to tackle things; that was the right spirit. Never say die; it was only a question of . . . But the fly had again finished its laborious task, and the boss had just time to refill his pen, to shake fair and square on the new-cleaned body yet another dark drop. What about it this time? A painful moment of suspense followed. But behold, the front legs were again waving; the boss felt a rush of relief. He leaned over the fly and said to it tenderly, "You artful little b . . ." And he actually had the brilliant notion of breathing on it to help the drying process. All the same, there was something timid and weak about its efforts now, and the boss decided that this time should be the last as he dipped the pen deep into the inkpot.

It was. The last blot fell on the soaked blotting-paper, and the draggled fly lay in it and did not stir. The back legs were stuck to the body; the front legs were not to be seen.

"Come on," said the boss. "Look sharp!" And he stirred it with his pen—in vain. Nothing happened or was likely to happen. The fly was dead.

The boss lifted the corpse on the end of the paper-knife and flung it into the waste-paper basket. But such a grinding feeling of wretchedness seized him that he felt positively frightened. He started forward and pressed the bell for Macey.

"Bring me some fresh blotting-paper," he said sternly, "and look sharp about it." And while the old dog padded away he fell to wondering what it was he had been thinking about before. What was it? It was. . . . He took out his handkerchief and passed it inside his collar. For the life of him he could not remember.

It's easy to interpret this gesture over-simply: the boss's grief has moved him to do violence to a harmless fly. But the delicate shifts in the boss's emotions and his responses to the fly's struggle move us beyond this surface reading to consider the distractions of casual cruelty, the pleasures of playing god as a means of mediating one's own sense of powerlessness, and the perverse desire to pass pain on to anyone—anything—who is weaker and more helpless than we are.

Though both scenes involve the murder of insects, the boss's fatal encounter with the fly couldn't be more unlike this moment near the beginning of Edward St. Aubyn's *Some Hope.* This massacre is being carried out by the young hero's sadistic father, Doctor David Melrose, and observed by the family maid, Yvette, who is carrying a heavy load of laundry that she ironed the night before.

> In his blue dressing gown, and already wearing dark glasses although it was still too early for the September sun to have risen above the limestone mountain, he directed a heavy stream of water from the hose he held in his left hand onto the column of ants moving busily through the gravel at his feet. His technique was well-established: he would let the survivors struggle over the wet stones, and regain their dignity for a while, before bringing the thundering water down on them again. With his free hand he removed a cigar from his mouth, its smoke drifting up through the brown and gray curls that covered the jutting bones of his forehead. He then narrowed the jet of water with his thumb to batter more effectively an ant on whose death he was wholly bent.
>
> Yvette had only to pass the fig tree and she could slip into the house without Doctor Melrose knowing she had arrived. His habit, though, was to call her without looking up from the ground just when she thought she was screened by the tree. Yesterday he had talked to her for long enough to exhaust her arms, but not for so long that she might drop the linen. He gauged such things very precisely.

Unlike the boss, who does not begin his spontaneous little contest with the fly until the insect has suffered an unfortunate accident, Doctor Melrose (and by now the close reader will have admired the way St. Aubyn has found to apprise us of the doctor's age and social class) is employing a well-established technique. The ants have done nothing to deserve their fate, nor do their struggles move him to the sort of admiration felt by the boss in the Mansfield story. In fact, he prolongs and intensifies their death, on which he is "wholly bent." So it hardly comes as a surprise when, in the next paragraph, we see him tiring of his game with the ants and redirecting his cruelty higher up the evolutionary ladder, tormenting a fellow human as he calculates the exact length of conversation required to make Yvette's arms ache from holding the heavy laundry but not causing her to drop it.

Usually we think of dialogue and physical description as the principal ways in which characters are created, but there are some writers who—when we stop and analyze their narrative strategies—turn out to rely heavily on gesture and on semiconscious action, especially when they are dealing with semirational and irrational fictive personalities. In the first chapter of Flannery O'Connor's novel *Wise Blood*, the God-haunted preacher Hazel Motes finds himself among the more ordinary travelers in the dining car of a train. Notice how dialogue is used to punctuate the lengthy catalogue of small actions, how dialogue serves as the punch line for the running jokes set by gesture:

> The steward beckoned and Mrs. Hitchcock and the women walked in and Haze followed them. The man stopped him and said, "Only two," and pushed him back to the doorway.
>
> Haze's face turned an ugly red. He tried to get behind the next person and then he tried to get through the line to go back to the car he had come from but there were too many people bunched in the opening. He had to stand there while everyone looked at him. No one left for a while. Finally a woman at the far end of the car got up and the steward jerked his hand. Haze hesitated and saw the hand jerk again. He lurched up the aisle, falling against two tables on the way and getting his hand wet in somebody's coffee. The steward placed him with three youngish women dressed like parrots.
>
> Their hands were resting on the table, red-speared at the tips. He sat down and wiped his hand on the tablecloth. He didn't take off his hat. The women had finished eating and were smoking cigarettes. They stopped talking when he sat down. He pointed to the first thing on the menu and the steward, standing over him, said, "Write it down, sonny," and winked at one of the women; she made a noise in her nose. He wrote it down and the steward went away with it. He sat and looked in front of him, glum and intense, at the neck of the woman across from him. At intervals her hand holding the cigarette would pass the spot on her neck; it would go out of his sight and then it would pass again,

going back down to the table; in a second a straight line of smoke would blow in his face. After it had blown at him three or four times, he looked at her. She had a bold game-hen expression and small eyes pointed directly at him.

"If you've been redeemed," he said, "I wouldn't want to be." Then he turned his head to the window. He saw his pale reflection with the dark empty space outside coming through it. A boxcar roared past, chopping the empty space in two, and one of the women laughed.

"Do you think I believe in Jesus?" he said, leaning toward her and speaking almost as if he were breathless. "Well I wouldn't even if He existed. Even if He was on this train."

"Who said you had to?" she asked in a poisonous Eastern voice. He drew back.

The waiter brought his dinner. He began eating slowly at first, then much faster as the women concentrated on watching the muscles that stood out on his jaw when he chewed. He was eating something spotted with eggs and livers. He finished that and drank his coffee and then pulled his money out. The steward saw him but he wouldn't come total the bill. Every time he passed the table, he would wink at the women and stare at Haze. . . . Finally the man came and added up the bill. Haze shoved money at him and then pushed past him out of the car.

Often, gestures betray the unconscious, but in fact there are many cases in which we are all too conscious of our gestures—and that consciousness too is a sort of revelation. In Beckett's work, characters are painfully aware of every move they make or don't make, just as they are conscious of everything—and nothing—about themselves. And much of Turgenev's novella *First Love* is told through the character's gestures, countless tiny actions that the narrator is too young and innocent to interpret correctly or understand.

The first time the narrator sees Zinaida, his neighbor, a beautiful young woman with whom he will fall in love, she is surrounded by four suitors. She is tapping them on the forehead with small gray flowers, a gesture that defines Zinaida's character (at least at that moment) and her relations with the men who adore her.

The young men presented their foreheads so eagerly, and there
was in the movements of the young girl . . . something so
fascinating, imperious, caressing, mocking and charming that I
nearly cried out with wonder and delight and would, I believe,
have given everything in the world at that moment to have those
lovely fingers tap me on the forehead too.

That night, the newly infatuated boy finds himself, without knowing why, spinning around three times before going to bed. Soon after, his friendship with Zinaida deepens—she draws him into her web, so to speak—when she asks him to hold the skein of red wool she is winding into a ball.

In one wordless scene, the narrator, strolling in his garden, coughs to attract his pretty neighbor's attention, then watches as she puts down the book she is reading to watch his father go by. The next day, Zinaida and her mother come for dinner, during which the strong current of attraction between Zinaida and the narrator's father becomes apparent to everyone but the narrator. Again, nothing needs to be said, no dialogue is required or reported. All that the narrator's mother has to observe in order to conceive an instant dislike for Zinaida is the way the young guest and her host behave at the table:

My father sat beside her during dinner and entertained his
neighbor with his usual exquisite and calm courtesy. From time to
time, he glanced at her, and she too looked at him now and again,
but so strangely, almost with hostility. Their conversation was
carried on in French; I remember I was surprised by the purity of
Zinaida's pronunciation.

Subsequently, all of Zinaida's gestures—mysterious smiles, enigmatic sighs, fevered handclasps—will be examined by the narrator for signs of love and favor, even as the reader knows that they are the actions of a woman in love with the father of a boy whose eyes remind her of his father's. And when the boy tells his father about a visit to Zinaida, we read a similar subtext in the father's response.

He listened to me half attentively and half absently, sitting on
a bench and drawing in the sand with the end of his riding crop.

From time to time he would chuckle, look at me in a sort of
bright and amused way, and he egged me on with short questions
and rejoinders.

That evening, the narrator visits Zinaida, who refuses to
see him and merely stares at him from her room, softly closes
the door, and refuses to respond when her mother calls her. And
the narrator's fate is sealed: "My passion began from that day."

Zinaida bites a blade of grass, asks to hear poetry read
aloud, blushes over a line or verse, twists the narrator's hair till
it hurts, asks him to jump down from a high wall, flings her
parasol into the dust, covers his face with kisses, pulls down her
window shade late one night after the narrator has seen his
father disappear in the direction of her house. Unbeknownst
to the boy, each of these gestures charts the trajectory of her
affair with his father. And all of it culminates in the celebrated
scene that the narrator watched from a distance, in silence. The
interlude plays out almost as if it were in pantomime, con-
ducted entirely through gestures except for one line of over-
heard dialogue.

It begins when the boy observes his father standing at an
open window of a small wooden house, talking to Zinaida,
who sits inside the window:

> *My father seemed to be insisting on something. Zinaida*
> *would not agree. . . . She did not raise her eyes but just smiled,*
> *submissively and obstinately. It was by this smile alone that*
> *I recognized my Zinaida as I used to know her. My father*
> *shrugged and set his hat straight on his head, which was always a*
> *sign of impatience with him. Then I heard the words: "Vous devez*
> *vous séparer de cette . . ." Zinaida drew herself up and stretched*
> *out her hand. . . . Suddenly something quite unbelievable took*
> *place before my very eyes; my father all of a sudden raised his*
> *riding crop, with which he had been flicking the dust from the*
> *skirts of his coat, and I heard the sound of a sharp blow across*
> *her arm, which was bared to the elbow. I just managed to restrain*
> *myself from crying out, while Zinaida gave a start, looked at my*
> *father without uttering a word, and, raising her arm to her lips,*
> *kissed the scar that showed crimson on it. My father flung away*

the crop and, running up the steps rapidly, rushed into the house. Zinaida turned round, tossed back her head, and, with arms outstretched, also moved away from the window.

This gesture—Zinaida kissing the welt on her arm—is what the narrator realizes will remain forever imprinted on his memory, together with the sexually charged reconciliation suggested by the father's haste and his mistress's outstretched arms. And that is certainly what remains with the reader.

Even the greatest writers may use stock gestures or employ gesture badly. Dickens sometimes includes gestures that are not so much revelations of personality as handy mnemonic devices designed to help us to keep track of a large cast of characters: this one blinks, that one twitches, this one limps, that one repeats the same phrase again and again. And of course, it's possible to write without describing gesture. One notices how rarely—almost never—Jane Austen uses physical gesture; perhaps her attention is so attuned to the shifts in a character's sensibility that she simply can't be bothered to lower her gaze and record the silly or pointless self-betrayals that the character's hands and feet, knees and elbows are performing.

If we are to see gesture—and why wouldn't we use this practical tool, this shortcut, this neat way of circumventing brain and mouth and proceeding directly to the heart—how can we use it more effectively? First of all, it's important, as with every word we write, to be careful and sparing. If a gesture is not illuminating, simply leave it out, or try cutting it and see if you later miss it or even remember that it's gone. Do we really need that cigarette lit, that glass of wine poured? Is it merely a way of passing time, of making space in dialogue, of telegraphing mood and emotion? Does it tell us something specific about the character or the situation we are attempting to recreate on the page?

And how do we find these telling gestures? The answer is, simply, by observation: by paying attention to the world. Watch people, watch them closely, and write down or remember what you see. (It might be argued that the recording of small gesture rather than the Big Idea is a more worthwhile use for one's empty notebook.) Notice that woman across from us on the subway compulsively fingering the tiny, almost imperceptible roll of flesh at her middle. Watch the young couple in the car pulled alongside us at the stop sign, the man performing an elaborate ballet with his head and hands to the rap song on the radio, the woman turned away from him, staring out the window.

In pursuit of what he called "the poetry of gesture," Proust cultivated what his housekeeper, Celestine Albert, called his

> *fabulous powers of observation and a tenacious memory. For example, each of the two or three times he looked through the kitchen window of rue Hamelin at Mm. Standish and her family at dinner, he made only a brief appearance, as if he were just passing by. But in thirty seconds everything was recorded, and better than a camera could do it, because behind the image itself there was often a whole character analysis based on a single detail—the way someone picked up a salt cellar, an inclination of the head, a reaction he had caught on the wing.*

Since I started off by criticizing bad actors and their stagy gestures, perhaps I should conclude by praising good actors, who are, after all, students of physical motion. Actors are always watching, and writers can learn by watching actors: the very different gestures that, let's say, Robert DeNiro uses to portray Jake LaMotta or Travis Bickle or any of the unkindly priests that he so often winds up playing. An actor once told me that years ago he had watched an old man caught in the rain without an umbrella and that he had later used the old man's hunched, defensive walk in portraying a father bowed by grief over the sudden death of a child.

Finally, I'd like to quote a story about gesture, about the attention a director might pay to the way that humans reveal their secrets in every move they make. The story, which is from a memoir by the actress Isabella Rossellini, is interesting to compare with a similar situation in fiction, one from L. P. Hartley's novel, *The Go-Between*. In both cases, the use of gesture involves an action that betrays or conceals a secret love affair.

The Hartley passage concludes a scene in which an aristocratic young Englishwoman is accompanying, on the piano, a post-cricket-match serenade sung by a local farmer, who, unbeknownst to the other guests, happens to be her lover:

> At the conclusion of the song there was a call for the accompanist, and Marian left her stool to share the applause with Ted. Half turning, she made him a little bow. But he, instead of responding, twice jerked his head round towards her and away again, like a comedian or a clown wisecracking with his partner. The audience laughed and I heard Trimingham say, "Not very gallant, is he?" My companion was more emphatic. "What's come over our Ted," he whispered across me to our other neighbor, "to be so shy with the ladies? It's because she comes from the Hall, that's why." Meanwhile Ted had recovered himself sufficiently to make Marian a bow. "That's better," my companion commented. "If it weren't for the difference, what a handsome pair they'd make!"

By contrast, Rossellini describes how an outer *show* of affection (rather than restraint) can be employed to conceal a passion. Shocked and grief-stricken at having been abandoned by her lover, David Lynch, the actress called her former husband Martin Scorsese to tell him what had happened:

> "Martin, David left me," I said on the phone.
> "I knew it," he announced to my complete surprise.
> "How did you know? None of us knew—none of my friends, none of my family expected it, and it was the furthest thing from my mind. How did you know?"
> "I knew it when I saw you and David on the news, at the Cannes Film Festival. When David won the Palme d'Or for Wild at Heart, he kissed you on the lips in front of the press."
> "So what?"
> "Well, you've both been so very discreet about your relationship, even if everybody knew you were together—there haven't been any photos, any declarations. If David chose to display his love to you in front of the press after the five years you were together, he obviously had something to hide."

BILLY COLLINS is the author of eight books of poetry, including *Ballistics, The Trouble with Poetry and Other Poems, Nine Horses, Sailing Alone around the World, Picnic, Lightning,* and *Questions about Angels,* which was selected by Edward Hirsch for the National Poetry Series. He is also the editor of *Poetry 180: A Turning Back to Poetry* and *180 More: Extraordinary Poems for Every Day.* Collins's poetry has appeared in anthologies, textbooks, and a variety of periodicals, including *Poetry, Harper's,* the *American Poetry Review,* the *American Scholar,* the *Paris Review,* and the *New Yorker.* His work has been included frequently in *The Best American Poetry.* He has received fellowships from the New York Foundation for the Arts, the National Endowment for the Arts, and the Guggenheim Foundation. He served as United States Poet Laureate from 2001 to 2003 and as New York State Poet from 2004 to 2006.

Collins was a featured writer at the 2006 Ohio University Spring Literary Festival.

The Myth of Craft

Thoughts on the Writing of Poetry

BILLY COLLINS

(you can tell this is going to be a scholarly presentation), said that the adjective is the enemy of the noun. The writer falsely believes that the noun by itself, standing alone, will not suffice. The poor noun has been standing naked all these years—centuries, really—waiting for the writer to come along and put the right clothes on it. But, in fact, the noun is just fine without the writer, just as the world itself is fine without the writer. The noun is actually closer to the thing it stands for than the writer will ever be because all the noun ever does is represent the thing. It's its only job. The word "apple" is tighter with the apple on the table than the writer will ever be no matter how hard he stares at it wondering how this piece of fruit can improve his position in literary society.

Emerson calls the self-sufficiency of objects "the speaking language of things," which implies that things—especially things found in Nature—are talking already without our help, our misconstrued desire to assist them in articulating themselves. They are not mute according to Emerson. It was Emerson who also said that we should act as if other people really existed because who knows? They just might. Which gives me even more reason to trust in Emerson's existence and his assertion that the things of the world enjoy a refreshing independence from us, and that includes people with agendas that involve self-expression. The toadstool does not need your adjective. The goldfish was fine before you showed up with your thesaurus and your envelopes, hopefully stamped and self-addressed. The streetlight wants to be left alone. So do the leaf and the blanket even if we find it nearly irresistible to make the leaf green and the blanket—I don't know—blue?

And as if one smothering modifier is not enough, double and triple adjectives may be deployed to finish the job. They gang up on the poor noun, drag it into an alley and beat the life out of it. The bullying modifier. Too strong a metaphor? Ok, then just some snails attached to the hull, slowing down the boat.

No contemporary writer likes to think he or she is part of a writing fad. Surely, the point of literature has been to arrive at this point in literary history and remain there. After all, so much is at stake for the writer, for committing acts of literature involves conveying a Zeitgeist, expressing one's Weltschmerz, and unleashing the inner flood of consciousness itself. But the fact is that verbal fashions do change, and at one time the generous release of modifiers into writing was an indispensable part of a literary performance. We need look no further than this sample, a sonnet from a poet, one of whose poems graces the base of the Statue of Liberty:

Long Island Sound
(EMMA LAZARUS)

I see it as it looked one afternoon
In August,—by a fresh, soft breeze o'erblown.
The swiftness of the tide, the light thereon,
A far-off sail, white as a crescent moon.
The shining waters with pale currents strewn,
The quiet fishing smacks, the Eastern cove,
The semi-circle of its dark, green grove.
The luminous grasses, and the merry sun
In the grave sky; the sparkle far and wide,
Laughter of unseen children, cheerful chirp
Of crickets, and low lisp of rippling tide,

Light summer clouds fantastical as sleep
Changing unnoted while I gazed thereon.
All these fair sounds and sights I made my own.

You have heard of the man who mistook his wife for a hat?
This poet has mistaken a body of water for a Christmas tree. If
you took all the nouns from the poem—breeze, tide, sail, moon,
waters, currents, cove, sun, sky, children, crickets, cloud (which is
kind of an impressionistic poem in itself)—and lined them up
on one side of the page, then took all the modifiers—fresh, soft,
far-off, shining, pale, quiet, luminous, merry, cheerful (which is
a really bad poem at best)—and lined them up on the opposite
side of the page, you would have the makings of a good gang
war, a rumble, the Sharks and the Jets, the Crips and the Bloods,
the Adjectives and the Nouns. The smart money is on the Nouns.

For comparison sake, here is a poem that is interested not
in cake decoration but in statement and is 100% modifier free,
guaranteed.

Keeping Things Whole
(MARK STRAND)

In a field
I am the absence
Of field.
This is
Always the case.
Wherever I am
I am what is missing.

When I walk
I part the air
And always
The air moves in
To fill the spaces
Where my body's been.

We all have reasons
For moving.
I move
To keep things whole.

Yet surely something positive can be said for the adjective, but what? Attaching an adjective to a noun just for the sake of demonstrating that you are a writer is an act of concealment, but turning a noun into its adjective can be revealing. The generally good connotations of "poetic" and the definitively bad ring in the word "prosaic" remind us of the superiority of poetry to prose. Poetry, after all, is a bird, and prose, as we know, is a potato. Nice that we can all agree on something.

Which brings us to "craft" and "crafty." "Craft" means skill, dexterity, a kind of knowledge, at least a useful knack. But "crafty" means sly, wily, underhanded, not to be trusted. Plus "craft" can turned into the longer and totally honorific word "craftsmanship." Coach and furniture makers come to mind. Which is just another reminder of how slippery language is in our wet hands, how it is often more complex than our self-expressive intentions, too elusive for its and our own good. Notice this: to teach someone English as a second language carries among its responsibilities the obligation to point out that the phrase "to take care of someone" means both to nurse and comfort that person and to kill him. Florence Nightingale takes care of a person much differently than Paulie Walnuts takes care of a person.

◆

IT TAKES AN adult to understand the craft of poetry, but to write a poem you must be part child, or at least not have lost entirely the capacity for childishness. How can anyone be both at once? That is an interesting paradox, and it is worth trying to work it out because poetry insists on asking its practitioners to do lots of contradictory things at the same time. You do not have to practice walking and chewing gum at the same time, but it takes concentration to write good sentences *and* good lines at the same time. And of course, the original double-demand of formal poetry is that the poet maintain a rhythm like a drummer while landing on a rhyme word at just the right moment like a singer perfectly hitting a note. Thus the poet has to keep the balls of cadence and sound, syntax and lineation up in the air throughout. Are these unreasonable demands? So it would appear, which must have moved an insightful and unabashed student of mine in a freshman literature class to say "Professor Collins, poetry is harder than writing."

We can add that poetry also offers regular opportunities to be in two contrary states of mind at once. Good poems are often playful and serious at the same time. Serious content/ playful style is the most common type of distribution. No matter how dark the subject—death, of course, is popular with us—a good poem will always convey a sense of linguistic play. A poet writing an elegy for your father might find himself poking around in the dictionary just to make sure he knows the difference between "luminous" and "numinous." Also, a poem can use clear language to achieve mysterious ends and access elusive places. Again, how do you manage to walk on both sides of the street at the same time? The answer is probably by not thinking about it very much.

I have noticed that when poets offer a succinct definition of poetry, they stress the genre's doubleness, its way of bringing normally opposed states into harmony and thereby making double demands on the writer. Here are a few examples:

Thomas Carlyle calls poetry "musical thought," an epithet that puts poetry at the intersection of thinking and singing. Usually, these acts are done separately. For Thomas Hardy poetry is "emotion set to measure," a condition that seems to demand that we keep a certain beat while being overwhelmed with strong feeling. Muriel Rukeyser says poetry is "meaning that moves," once again combining the conceptual and the rhythmic. An idea somehow in motion. Philosophy meets choreography. And Kenneth Burke simply puts this view another way when he claims that poetry is "the dancing of an attitude." Common to these definitions is an acknowledgment that poetry *animates* thought and feeling.

Whether it is "the best words in the best order" (Coleridge) or "the synthesis of hyacinths and biscuits" (MacLeish), definitions of poetry rely not just on paradox but on the conviction that poetry can resolve a dialectic by throwing open the door that separates the two rooms of the bicameral brain. The poet feels while he is counting. The poet has to think while she dances. The poet is asked to juggle knives and Ping-Pong balls at the same time.

Irresistible to me while we are on the subject, here are a few attempts to define poetry by illustration. Christopher Ricks gives the example of "the silence of the green fields" (prose) and "the green silence of the fields" (poetry). "I have no idea why I'm crying" would be prose, whereas "Tears, idle tears, I know not what they mean" would have the sound and pace of poetry. And Kenneth Koch perhaps takes the cake here when he says prose is "No dogs allowed on the beach" but poetry is "No dogs or logs allowed on the beach / No poodle however trim / no dachshund unable to swim."

So: poetry, it would appear, is a self-contradictory genre that makes a complex set of unreasonable demands on anyone who wants to be considered a poet. But there is a way around all these requirements and double-demands, which brings us to the secret message I am here to deliver. Simply put, you get someone else to do it for you. And that fellow is known in the glossaries of literary terms as a *persona*. Every successful poet has a persona they invented to make their lives easier and, in addition, to make them appear to be better human beings than they actually are. Sharon Olds has one. Mary Oliver has one. So do Galway Kinnell and James Tate. We all have one, which is why meeting us is so disappointing. If you are a novelist or a playwright, a major part of your work is the invention of characters, each one distinct from the others. Hyperprolific novelists like Trollope, Balzac, and Joyce Carol Oates have to invent hundreds of characters, and the same goes for playwrights with the breadth of Shakespeare, Molière, or O'Neill. But—and here is the best news I have for you—if you are a poet, all you have to do over the course of a lifetime of writing is come up with one single character. In the classroom we commonly call this entity a "persona" or "the speaker," but like characters in fiction and drama, the persona has a definite personality. You cannot spell "personality" without "persona." Such a character most likely resembles the poet to some degree or a great degree but is not the exact equivalent of the poet. I believe William Matthews said that the voice that spoke his poems was not exactly his voice, but it bore a closer resemblance to his voice than to anyone else's on earth.

Typically, the persona is like the poet, only better. A definite improvement. For the persona is just another part of that complex exercise in wish-fulfillment called literature. Your persona, if you manage to come up with one, is your better. His or her life is simpler and more noble than yours. My persona, for example, has never had a job; he has never set foot in a laundromat and plans never to do so. He has never had to untangle a mess of Christmas tree lights. My persona is a vast improvement over the actual Billy Collins. He never stays out too late, he's never been to a driving range, and he never sits around googling himself. No, my persona is too busy writing poems, which is what he is supposed to be doing.

There is no hope for you unless you have a persona. Once you have your persona in place, craft becomes a simple affair, a transparency, no problem, as they say when they hand you your change. Of course, you can devote yourself to an academic study of craft, and you might even learn something useful about which kind of stanza goes with which kind of poem and how to come up with a title that won't frighten your readers away. You can break down poetry into its moving parts, but all this knowledge is relatively useless without a persona. That is because craft—don't go spreading this around—craft is really just the mannerisms that characterize your persona. It's just the way he or she speaks. Once you have your persona down, you never again have to give craft another thought. Nor does your persona, because for your persona, all craft boils down to is figuring out what the next line will be. Line by line, and then knowing which one is the last one, and then it's time to stop. The persona is the internalization of craft.

Now at this point you might ask: what am I supposed to be doing while my persona is busy writing? You are supposed to be listening, because now you have become your persona's audience. And it's your job to tell the persona how he or she sounds. Give him or her a little feedback. Another name for that is *editing*. Eventually in your career, if you are lucky or unlucky, people will begin calling you a poet. But you will know that, in fact, you are not a writer nor do you have an audience. You have something better. You have a persona, who has become the writer, and you have become his or her audience, his or her first reader.

PETER HO DAVIES is the author of the novel *The Welsh Girl* and the story collections *The Ugliest House in the World* and *Equal Love.* His work has appeared in *Harper's,* the *Atlantic Monthly,* the *Paris Review,* and *Granta* (which in 2003 named him as one of the "Best of Young British novelists"), and his short fiction has been widely anthologized, including selections for *Prize Stories: The O. Henry Awards* and *Best American Short Stories.* A recipient of fellowships from the Guggenheim Foundation and the National Endowment for the Arts, he was awarded a 2008 PEN/Malamud Prize for excellence in the short story.

Davies was a featured writer at the 2009 Ohio University Spring Literary Festival.

Only Collect

Something about the
Short Story Collection

PETER HO DAVIES

I WAS CHATTING TO ANOTHER parent outside my son's preschool, recently, while we waited for our kids to come out. I was alone, she had another child, a girl of about seven or eight, twisting and twirling at the end of her hand.

The mother, it turned out, had read my novel in her book group and wanted to know what else I'd written. I muttered something about my couple of collections, experience having taught me that telling someone who knows you're a novelist that you also have story collections is at best underwhelming and a worst strikes them as irrelevant, a little like asking LeBron James what other games he loves, and having him reply, Canasta.

I was starting to talk, a bit more brightly, about my novel-in-progress, when the little girl piped up, "*What* do you collect?" She hadn't been paying attention before, but she'd intuited awkwardness from the way I'd lowered my voice to talk about my collections and—like an animal scenting weakness—pricked up her ears. "What are your two collections?"

she asked again, this time with a touch of challenge in her voice, and I was about to say, lamely, "Stories" (if only to clear myself of the even more mortifying possibility that I wrote poetry!), when her mother broke in and told her, "Oh dear, they're not that kind of collection."

"*I* collect Beanies," the girl told me, firmly, "*and* Hummels *and* erasers *and* ponies. I've got all kinds, from all over." I wasn't sure if she meant the Beanie Babies, or the ponies, but her pride, her foursquare satisfaction of possession, left me with little doubt that she considered noncollectors with a touch of pity, and would likely find the idea of a collection of stories *I'd written myself* not only dull, but akin to cheating.

"It's the age of collecting," her mother advised me, as the kids emerged from the school. "Yours will be at it soon enough."

◆

THEY'RE NOT THAT *kind of collection.* I trade in such parental evasions all the time, and the mother was clearly just trying to shield me politely from her daughter's badgering. And yet the phrase stuck in my craw, a little, along with my own inability to answer her daughter's question. (No writer after all likes someone else to speak for him.) In truth, though, I largely agreed with the mother—my collections *aren't* that kind of collection. But, of course, what really nagged me is the question, *what kinds of collections are they, then?*

◆

I HAVE BEEN talking to my students for a few years about different types of story collections, based on my own experiences with the form. My first book, *The Ugliest House in the World,* for instance, was assembled under the not very edifying organizing principle of "all the good stuff I happen to have right now." I don't mean to entirely dismiss this kind of collection. I believe that one of the strengths of collections (and one of the pleasures of writing stories generally) is that they can be very diverse. Story by story a writer can change subject, tone, style, point of view, you name it, with much more freedom than, say, a novelist. In my own case, I should confess that this aesthetic arises from pragmatism. I've tended to consciously write very different stories as a means of escaping the hangover from earlier stories—the way the first draft of a new story always seems so dreadful compared to the final draft of a previous story. It's an unfair comparison, of course, but an inevitable one, and my means of tricking myself past this particular writer's block has been to make sure that the next story is as far as possible incommensurable with the last—if one was light, the next will be dark, if one was contemporary, the next will be historical, if one was in first person, the next will be in third, etc., etc.

Collections of such varied work, of course, risk the dreaded verdict of being "uneven" (a friend of mine argues that there are actually only two reviews of short story collections, "promising mixed bag" for a first collection, and plain old "mixed bag" for a later one), but I'm inclined to admire those varied collections in which we inevitably love some stories and hate others as works in which the writer has maximized the potential range of the form.

Such radical variety may also serve to distinguish the collection from the novel in another way. I was reading a review a few years ago in which a particularly famous contemporary novel was being described as essentially the best thing since sliced bread—the critical consensus on this book, in fact. According to the reviewer, it was terrific in this way, wonderful in that way, "but, of course," the reviewer noted, almost in passing, "it falls apart at the end." Think about that for a moment. This reviewer, I'm certain, was sincerely of the opinion that the novel was wonderful, and yet also recognized *it fell apart at the end*. The comment stayed with me, probably, because it resonated with the way I felt about several contemporary novels (I'm not going to name names)—really fine works that nonetheless disappointed in their endings. But perhaps that's not too surprising. Novels, in the most basic sense, whether we're talking about Jane Austen or John Grisham, are machines to make us keep reading. If we love a novel, again irrespective of genre, we're apt to say things like "I couldn't put it down," "I stayed up all night to finish it," "I couldn't stop turning the pages." The most fundamental novelistic skill, one might argue, is the ability to keep us reading, which perhaps explains why novelists—even gifted ones—aren't great at endings, at stopping us reading. But now consider that idea, *it's a great novel, but it falls apart at the end,* and imagine, for a moment, saying it about a story. I don't think you can, right? If a story falls apart at the end, it's not a great story, it's not even a mediocre story, it's just *bad*. Though, on the contrary, we might say of a story that the "ending makes it" (something said much less often about novels, because if only the ending makes it few readers may get that far to find out). A short story lives or dies by its ending. And if that ending is good enough, it should also be sufficient. It should suspend you, hold you, satisfy you to such an extent that you don't want to turn the page, read another story immediately. Thus the discontinuities of varied, even haphazardly assembled collections like my own first book might actually be in concert with this idea of stories as what Lorrie Moore has called an "end-based form."

◆

FOR ALL THAT, though, it's not hard to imagine an eight-year-old girl being unimpressed by such a collection. True, the constituents are all of the same kind—stories—and there's an important notion that while related they should also be varied, but this interest in similarity and difference, and especially the differences within similarity and the similarity within difference, is a basic tenet of any collection (we can assume that little girl collected *different* Beanies, for instance, and we would find it odd, even creepy, if she collected identical ones). Such a collection as my first book is a little like presenting the first dozen or so stones that catch your eye on a beach and saying, "Here's my rock collection." The only choice such a collection offers, beyond the initial selection, is how it is presented—in the case of a story collection, how it is ordered. That can, as we'll see, be a very subtle question, but only when the individual elements have a complex relation to one another. In the case of my first collection my editor gave me some pointed advice: "Put the best story first, and the second best last. The critics may only read those." She didn't say, she was too polite to, but the corollary of such an argument is that you try to bury weaker stories somewhere in the middle of a collection, or at the very least try to disguise your weaknesses (an overreliance on first person, say, or present tense, or death) by trying to space out the stories that lean on such devices and material. That's a valuable defensive organization, to be sure, but hardly an aesthetically interesting one.

◆

OF COURSE, I'M doing my first collection a bit of a disservice here. There are other links between the stories—an interest in identity, most notably—which I'd only been semiconscious of myself but which several readers and critics noted. This, of course, is one of the great pleasures of collecting one's work, and one of my pleasures as a teacher in working with graduate students who are assembling theses. That act of collection is often a seminal moment in the development of such writers. They go from being people who write stories, to people who write books, and most important, in setting their stories side by side, in considering them collectively, they gain new insight into their work, new perspectives on it, frequently discovering things in the work that they were previously unconscious of. Some of these things, as noted above, can be weaknesses—an overuse or predilection for certain images, certain modes of storytelling—but many others suggest recurring obsessions or interests that the writer himself is un- or only dimly aware of.

The assembling of a collection therefore seems like another step toward how we as writers read ourselves and our work, just as a workshop or giving a reading heightens and changes our relationship to our work because it allows us to stand back from it and apprehend it anew, often through the eyes or ears of readers. If the recurring weaknesses seem to narrow our work, these recurring strengths often deepen it, and can be built on. Old stories can be revised in light of one another—"stuck" stories can often be cracked open in this fashion—and thrillingly new stories can be prompted by old ones, to fill gaps in a collection.

◆

PERSONALLY, I WAS guided toward these potentials a little more brutally than I hope my students are. As I mentioned above, readers and reviewers are apt to make connections that the writer may have been only partially aware of, or indeed not have intended. Part of the reading act, I suspect, is to look for the logic in a collection, even when it may be capriciously composed. We're hard-wired to look for pattern, and to call a body of work a collection is to invite such scrutiny.

This was brought home to me in particular by one British review of my first book—a fairly complimentary review, I should stress—headlined, ahem, "Linked by Flatulence." (There is, to be fair, one story in which farting plays a major role and it's mentioned in two others—though in one of those cases the fart in question is a fake one.) The worst of it was that the caption under my friendly author photo read "Peter Ho Davies, what's he smiling about?" So . . . having learned the hard way that readers will find links even where they're not intended, I set out in my second collection, *Equal Love,* to shape and define the links between my stories, to write essentially the second and more interesting kind of collection, a linked collection—in my case a thematically linked collection concerned with the various relationships between parents and children. Such a collection immediately makes new demands, and the aesthetic of variation is given more purpose. In a gesture toward completeness I wanted to have stories about sons but also daughters, stories about fathers but also mothers, stories about young children but also adult children. Such links also necessarily suggest different ways of thinking about how stories are ordered—in the case of *Equal Love,* for instance, the child at the center of each story gets progressively older as the collection proceeds.

◆

THIS SECOND—LINKED—kind of collection is, of course, open to a vast range of interpretation, with the links capable of being articulated in multiple ways, of which *Equal Love* provides only one or two simple examples. It is possible, however, to discern some patterns or trends in the construction of most linked story collections (typically, strong collections will employ several of these linking strategies).

At the micro level we can make out small stitches of language between stories. Denis Johnson's *Jesus' Son* provides a beautiful example. In the first story of that book, "Car Crash While Hitch-Hiking," he offers a vivid description of a midwestern sky with "clouds like great grey brains," an image so striking we easily recall it almost a hundred pages later in a story called "The Other Man" where another sky is described as "as blue and brainless as the love of God." (Obviously, in a collection called *Jesus' Son*, recurring references to God, and especially to salvation, also knit the collection together thematically.) Other examples of these kinds of echoes can occur in adjacent stories. At the start of Hemingway's *In Our Time,* we find his famous story "Indian Camp," in which Nick Adams and his doctor-father travel to the Indian Camp of the title to tend to a pregnant woman, whose husband kills himself during her labor. The story is succeeded by "The Doctor and the Doctor's Wife," which starts with men from the Indian Camp reversing the journey of the earlier story by coming to the home of the doctor and *his* wife to cut logs. In Edward P. Jones's *Lost in the City* the second, widely anthologized story, "The First Day," about a young girl's first day at school, is followed by a story called "The Night Rhonda Ferguson Was Killed," which, while it ranges widely, opens with another older girl waiting at the gates of her high school. Such echoes of language and structure, of course, also imply comparisons and the possibility of contrasts. Joyce, for instance, ends successive stories in *Dubliners,* "A Little Cloud" and "Counterparts," with images of fatherhood. In the former, the protagonist Little Chandler, after a frustrating encounter over drinks with a more successful friend, finds himself at home, his wife out, with only his baby for company, and in the story's climax he ends up screaming at the poor child to stop crying. He is interrupted by his wife's return, and the mother rocks the baby in her arms while "tears of remorse" start in Chandler's eyes. In the following story we meet the even more stymied Farrington, who like Little Chandler returns home from a night of drinking with friends to find his wife out, and promptly beats—remorselessly, in this case—his young son (now one of five kids) for letting the fire go out. These stories suggest parallels, mirrorings, and even elements of pseudo narrative (a young girl grows into an older, albeit different one; a man's family grows from one child to five). There's a sense in which these echoing narratives of comparison and contrast offer alternatives to each other, and, not surprisingly, several writers have interpreted these alternatives in metafictional terms. Angela Carter in *The Bloody Chamber* offers two versions of the story of Little Red Riding Hood back to back in "Werewolves" and "The Company of Wolves," both revisions of each other and, of course, of the original tale. And Tim O'Brien in *The Things They Carried* (a hybrid of novel and collection, one might argue) offers multiple contradictory versions of several events.

Salinger takes this echoing quality and extends it across the span of a whole collection. *Nine Stories* opens famously with "A Perfect Day for Bananafish," which offers as its most memorable scene an encounter between the suicidal Seymour Glass and a pert young girl, Sybil. This encounter is echoed in the middle of the collection in "For Esmé—With Love and Squalor," where the narrator, Sergeant X, encounters another precocious young lady, though in this case Esmé seems eventually able to save the adult from his incipient breakdown. This sequence is brought to a telling close in the final story of the collection, "Teddy,'" where yet another precocious child, a boy this time and a professed genius, talks with another adult before calmly heading toward a death he has foreseen (a kind of suicide in its own right).

These links between pairs and small groups of stories begin to point the way toward overarching patterns that link all the stories in a collection. Joyce, from whom I and countless others borrow the chronological device of progressively aging central characters (*Dubliners* famously starts with stories about children, moves to those about adolescents and young adults, and progresses toward maturity and death), also offers us the idea of the collection as a community, something we see clearly too in *Winesburg, Ohio,* where the separateness of stories, the discontinuity I've talked about earlier, seems to suggest the limits of communication, the fundamental gaps between people, the very loneliness that, paradoxically, we all share. Community is explicitly addressed in several distinguished recent collections, too—Edward P. Jones's aforementioned *Lost in the City,* another of those that owes a conscious debt to *Dubliners,* and Jhumpa Lahiri's *Interpreter of Maladies.* Interestingly, in both of these, as in *Dubliners,* the community depicted is never unitary. Oh, our foreground attention is occupied by the citizens of Dublin, to be sure, but much of the talk is of the *other*—exotic distant lands like Araby, or the "Buenos Ayres" that Eveline is on the verge of journeying to, or the other closer to home—the London where Ignatius Gallaher, Little Chandler's friend, has made a home, or the Paris he has visited, the Europe of race cars and drivers in "After the Race" and of opera singers in "The Dead." Always behind these stories lies a tension between here and there, a tension made piquant by Joyce's frequently negative view of the here. *Dubliners* in this sense contains both Dublin and by implication not-Dublin, England, Europe, to the east, and also in the final image of "The Dead," where snow is "general all over Ireland," the rest of the country to the west. We might locate this sense of here and there in Joyce's own life, the life and biases of an exile looking back on a parochial home. Yet we can observe the same doubling of location in the work of Edward P. Jones, a committed Washingtonian who continues to live there. Jones's characters are deeply aware of both a here—the African American neighborhoods of DC—and a there. A couple of "theres" actually—one that is the south from which so many of these families or their forebears came (a history Jones explores in later stories in the collection like "A Dark Night" and "Marie" and carries forward into the first story of his next collection, "All Aunt Hagar's Children," which goes back in time to introduce one of the secondary characters from the first story of *Lost in the City* as a baby). But Jones is also aware of another "there," the "there" of white DC, rarely glimpsed but like the London and the English of *Dubliners* felt in their bones by his characters, some of whom are beginning to move into that territory, against the advice of the older generation, one of whom pointedly advises, "Never get lost in white folks' neighborhood" (just one of the many echoing references to getting lost that tie the collection together).

Lahiri's first collection is similarly concerned with community, but also the fragmentation of community. Her East Coast Bengali Americans are contrasted with Indians at home in Calcutta—in the title story most obviously where a vacationing family of Indian Americans is given a tour of a temple by a local guide. In each of these collections, then, characters are collected within a certain community, but each suggests a varied relation to or place within that community. Most notably, each of these communities—like the postwar Jewish American one in *Goodbye, Columbus*—is in a state of flux. These changes, these moves—geographical, or socioeconomic, or cultural—all imply a fragmenting of community, a whole that is also in parts, which seems especially well suited to the collection as a form, and perhaps suggests that the collection (as much as the story, as many have suggested) is an especially American form, a reflection of the melting pot.

Some of the communities of collections, however, are formed less by geography and ethnicity than by shared events. It's perhaps significant that several of the books I've already touched on are shaped by war—the First World War of *In Our Time,* the Second underpinning *Nine Stories,* Vietnam in *The Things They Carried.* War makes communities—of comrades, of survivors— while simultaneously destroying or fragmenting them, and the experience of these wars is in itself fragmentary for their participants. Vietnam for O'Brien is episodic, senseless—very fit material for a collection. As for Hemingway's war, it seems too vast to be more than glimpsed, and the cumulative effect of *In Our Time* is an almost cubist portrait of the conflict (one that ends in "Big Two-Hearted River" with Nick alone, going fishing, but first crossing the burnt-out landscape of a forest fire, which resonates with the shattered images of no-man's land he's left behind). As for Salinger, *Nine Stories* is more concerned with the fragmentary aftermath of war—the discontinuities of early death and especially suicide.

Several of the collections mentioned here are, of course, linked (and sometimes linked to other work by their authors) by recurring characters—Nick Adams, Seymour Glass, "Tim O'Brien" himself. But these individuals are typically part of a community—the Lost Generation, the Glass family, Alpha Company—in transition, or disillusion. In Edward Jones's DC community and Sherwood Anderson's Winesburg, characters who appear as minor figures in one story, part of the background community, recur as major players in another, or vice versa. Joyce, interestingly, eschews such links, a surprising choice since the Dublin of his day is a small town compared to a modern city and we might expect in such a teeming volume characters to bump up against each other. And yet, if we look at "The Dead," there's a sense in which it gathers up at its great holiday feast not the individuals we've encountered in past stories, but their types, their spirits, we might even say. The drunks, the serving girls, the literary men, the singers from the earlier stories all find their analogs around the table. Even the recurring individuals in these collections, though, are subject to fragmentation. It's significant perhaps that Denis Johnson's collection includes titles like "Two Men" and "The Other Man" and that mirrors play a recurring role in the stories (at one moment he writes of a mirror above a bar as "a knife dividing everything from itself," a terrific image that also happens to echo the most memorable image of the whole collection, a knife plunged into someone's eye). Lorrie Moore for her part has a story called "How to Be the Other Woman," and her use of second person in *Self-Help* is interesting in that her "You's" seem to simultaneously imply an effaced "I"—a double-voiced quality we see in many retrospective narrations where both the child's point of view and that of the adult looking back are suggested (Jones, for instance, deploys this strategy in "The First Day").

There are many other kinds of linked collection I might add to this catalog. One subset would include Angela Carter's *The Bloody Chamber* and Italo Calvino's *Cosmicomics,* works that seem to rely on master narratives (folktale and scientific theories respectively) to shape them, as others, including the wartime collections mentioned above, lean on our shared history. There are other devices I might touch on too—the shaping power of titles (*In Our Time,* say, which so provocatively implies even as it excludes the first word of the prayer for "*Peace in our time*") and even of epigraphs, like Salinger's famous use of the Zen koan, "What is the sound of one hand clapping?" at the start of *Nine Stories,* which seems to invite, even demand, a certain approach to the book as a whole. And of course, there's much that might be said of closing stories—the way they frequently approach age and death, after *Dubliners,* but also often reverse themselves and circle back to the start of the collection (youth and young love are evoked in "The Dead," after all, just as the dying woman, the title character Marie, in the final story of *Lost in the City* recalls her earliest arrival in DC).

◆

THIS SUMMARY OF the kinds of story collections, though necessarily limited, suggests some commonalities. An interest in variation—alternatives, mirrorings, parallels—within ostensive similarity (of community, ethnicity, experience), and perhaps too a desire to hold together or put back together that which has already begun to come apart. But I'm left with the question I began with. If these are some of the recurring attributes of story collections, how do they compare to a more general sense of collecting that that little girl at the start might share?

◆

MY OWN CHILDHOOD collections included key rings and embroidered patches, as well as those enthusiasms foisted upon most kids by well-meaning adults—coins, and stamps. Collections seemed important then. I can even recall that little girl's question—"What do you collect?"—said with just that edge of challenge, from my childhood. Because surely what we collect is a measure of who we are, our passions—an often conscious declaration of self. I'm someone who collects X. It's an individual image we project into the world and one we invite the world—friends, family, etc.—to corroborate by buying us more of whatever X is. Yet I always remember the question of what I collected, and the declaration that it required, making me uneasy as a child. Partly, there was an implicit threat—what if the other person collected what you collected and, worse, had more of it than you did? I was never much good at the competitive collecting of trading cards, never had parents who'd buy me more than one pack of gum at a time (my mother was a dentist, after all), never completed my "teams" of players before the end of a season. Even the act of collecting made me anxious—the problem with key rings and patches, for instance, is that they're almost infinitely varied. As a child, I think it dawned on me quite early that I'd doomed myself to collect these things for the rest of my life and that it was a Sisyphean task—uncompletable. And yet, a collection once begun is hard to disassemble, to throw away or break up. Somewhere in an old biscuit tin in my parents' attic those key rings are still waiting for me, begging for completion. Finally, I think my deepest fear was that I wouldn't have anything to say to the question, What do you collect? Deep down I suspected the real answer was nothing, but try telling that to an adult. It's abnormal, somehow, suggestive of some deficiency. Human beings are hunter-gatherers, after all—activities that are *both* implied by collecting.

With the possible exception of stories, I don't think I collect anything now. As we become older, I suppose, we're defined less by our collections than by our choices—what we major in, our jobs, our partners (though I guess there are those who collect the latter). Of course, like any writer I have the obligatory collection of rejection slips—but that's at best an ironic collection, one that in its very cliché perhaps is more about collecting ourselves up into the collection (or community) called writers. I also have a lot of pens—people do love to give writers pens (a gesture I find faintly nagging, somehow, as well as depressing in its lack of imagination). I even toyed with collecting antique fountain pens briefly after the gift of a couple—indeed I have writer friends who collect typewriters—but what was a lovely gift felt awkwardly precious as a choice of collection (though fountain pens and typewriters—those "ancient" tools of our trade—do suggest the recurrent nostalgia inherent in collecting). Of course, I do have a lot of things—a dismaying pile of possessions that has grown exponentially since I bought a house and stopped moving apartments every couple of years with the inevitable culls that entailed—and a lot of them are the same things, books most obviously. But I don't quite think of my books as a collection per se—not any more at least—perhaps because the books at my home are a blended set of mine and my wife's and thus don't speak to our individuality, perhaps because over the years the books have just accumulated in a random fashion—those read for that class, those read but not enjoyed, those given as gifts but never read, all diluting the essentialness of the collection. It's a far cry from the days in my teens when I would be thrilled to discover some series of science fiction novels and look forward not only to reading them, but to reading them all, and then lining up their identical spines on my bedroom shelf like trophies.

I confess that the one thing I am pretty thorough about collecting is me—my works, collecting my collections—even down to dogging my agent to get me a copy of a recent Italian edition of one of my books, which will eventually find a home on what my wife likes to call "my vanity shelf." But then as I said earlier we collect to define ourselves, our identities, and that seems as true of my vanity shelf as of my own collections of stories, as of any collection.

◆

STILL, THE SELF somehow seems a poor, unsatisfying note of commonality, especially when we're talking about collecting, which, while it might represent the self, also seems at its best more capacious, more embracing of the rest of the world.

Perhaps we need to open our idea of collections up even further. If we take, for the sake of argument, as our first collector, Noah, what does his example suggest to us about what makes a good collection? Noah in fact seems to offer an ideal of collecting. His collection is complete (or at least we're told so; I guess any creatures he left out aren't around to complain—collections in this sense have the power of inclusion and exclusion: the excluded is rendered invisible). We might call it representationally complete, in fact. He doesn't, can't, save every animal; he just saves two of every kind. His then is a complete sample. What are the other hallmarks of Noah's collection? It's a benign act, of course, an act of preservation, of salvation, indeed. Lastly, and perforce in Noah's case, but perhaps by choice for later collectors, Noah's collection is very varied, very diverse. It's not all of one thing; it's a grouping of disparate things with one thing in common (they can't swim).

Of course, there are other modes of collection, other choices. Noah might have decided to collect one animal, a whole herd of cattle, for instance. And we know of such collectors, we call them, well . . . monopolists. We see in their hoarding a motive of greed, a desire for power. If this kind of collection is about preservation it's about self-preservation. This evil collection is most obviously manifest in the Nazis' final solution, the desire to collect all Jews . . . in order to liquidate them. Perhaps this is why the diverse, representative, preserving collection is the one we aspire to.

◆

THERE ARE ECHOES here, too, of our story collections. Surely, the act of recording these stories of fragmenting communities is an effort at saving something, preserving something. We collect in order to *recollect,* perhaps. But the stumbling block is that idea of completion, surely. Noah gets to complete his collection. I, as a child, gave up on collections that seemed uncompletable. And yet, I continue to write and indeed to write collections (though my editors when I signed a deal recently for another novel and a collection made it abundantly clear that they were taking on the latter as a favor to me, one bound to lose money). But if completion is the ideal goal of collections, and we give up collections that can't be completed, what do story collections aspire to? We don't do it for the money, as the sales figures suggest, so what is the satisfaction?

Well, I'm reminded of a final example. "It's the age of collecting," that young mother told me. But collecting, in my experience, has two ages—childhood and old age. My father on retirement, say, started to collect, very systematically, an early form of trading card called cigarette cards that—as their name implies—were included with British cigarettes from the early twentieth century into the 1970s. He must have a couple of thousand sets—flags of the world, famous ships, inventors, Boy Scout badges, even famous authors—each card sealed in a little plastic window, snapped into a ring binder. For ten years after retirement he combed flea markets, antique shops, estate sales, bidding low and always driving hard bargains often for boxes of unsorted cards. My mother in his wake felt the need to start her own collection—of salters, the little bowls of salt that used to be placed on a dining table with a tiny spoon before salt shakers became the norm. Her collection petered out within a year or two, overwhelmed by her competing interests, reading, knitting, travel. But more surprisingly, his—which had been his *thing,* his passion—has also now in his seventies all but ground to a halt. He's got them all, essentially—or at least got all those that don't cost hundreds of pounds per card (his parsimoniousness, *his* coin collection, is perhaps more defining of who he is than any collection). And while a part of me is relieved—he could become a real tyrant on trips, hunting down antique shops at the expense of dinner, and overbearing in his demands that you ooh and aah over his latest finds—a part of me is also dismayed. He chose this activity for his retirement, a nostalgic return to his youth, of course, and now . . . it's finished. Something is "off" here. His collection is finished before him; the idea of completing a collection seems in this light filled with pathos. The completion of a collection speaks of passion spent, of death (remember how many collections end with death or at least its anticipation). Our last collection, if we're so lucky, after all, will be our *collected* stories, or poems, and those collectors who collect us, our signed first edition, will realize our worth only after our deaths.

◆

CONTRARY TO NOAH'S example, then, I'd argue that while we all *aspire* to completion, look forward to it, want to collect collections that could theoretically be completed, we don't actually want to complete them (that would be an end to the fun, after all). And story collections, I'd argue, do have this in common with other collections.

Each of the books I've talked about above balances the narrowing danger of repetition against the deepening possibilities of variation and echo. Perhaps most obviously, each evinces a tension between cohesion and fragmentation, between the parts and the whole, an acknowledgement of the fragility or temporary nature of the whole which harkens back to the idea of collections as a means of preservation, or at least of recording, and provides a contrast to the novel with its focus on the "new."

Collections in essence, then, speak to the very tenuous nature of completeness and thus thrive on comparison (consider my two titles, The *Ugliest* House in the World, *Equal* Love), on doublings, on reflection, on alternatives. Stories mirror each other, and parallel each other. The sense then is of completion implied, an imperfect or shadow completion, a completion through antithesis. Collections finally don't, can't, contain an entirety, and yet they invite us, the reader, to imagine it.

Which is perhaps where I should end this collection of thoughts about collections. A collection that started in childhood, approached death at its close, offered a range of alternatives in its midst, and that I hope has in its incompletion invited you to fill in its gaps.

And *that's* my kind of collection.

CHARLES BAXTER was born in Minneapolis
and graduated from Macalester College in
Saint Paul. After completing graduate work in
English at the State University of New York at
Buffalo, he taught for several years at Wayne
State University in Detroit. In 1989, he moved
to the Department of English at the University
of Michigan and its MFA program. He now
teaches at the University of Minnesota. Baxter is
the author of numerous short stories and poetry
collections, books about writing, and many
award-winning novels, including *First Light, The
Feast of Love, Saul and Patsy,* and *The Soul Thief.*

Baxter was a featured writer at the 1995 Ohio
University Spring Literary Festival.

Stillness

CHARLES BAXTER

> My work is rooted in silence. It grows out of
> deep beds of contemplation, where words,
> which are living things, can form and re-form
> into new wholes. What is visible, the finished
> books, are underpinned by the fertility of
> uncounted hours. A writer has no use for the
> clock. A writer lives in an infinity of days, time
> without end, ploughed under.
>
> It is sometimes necessary to be silent for months
> before the central image of a book can occur.
>
> —Jeanette Winterson, *Art Objects*

IT'S LATE AT NIGHT, AND YOU
are quarreling with someone on the telephone, long distance.
You have reached a stalemate of sorts, where nothing remains
to be said. You cannot hang up. But you cannot say anything
more. So you remain on the line. Neither of you utters a word.
A moment like this stirs the air with an odd and indefinable
feeling. It is not like the silence after a quarrel in a room, because AT&T is going to bill you (or the other person) for this
silence. This gap—this emotional and technological emptiness—is literally going to cost you.

In the days before fiber-optic technology, these moments
also happened to put you into the wash of background trans-
mission noise. Behind your mutual silence in the foreground

came the faraway hiss and gurgle of the wires. Sometimes, distantly, you could hear other conversations. Straining not to speak yourself, you might end up eavesdropping on someone's random casual happiness. You might hear laughter, laughter hundreds of miles away, still faintly audible.

The hiss and gurgle and the laughter are the markers of time moving through stillness.

◆

IN ONE OF his film reviews, James Agee refers to "expressive air-pockets of dead silence." The reference is to intentional gaps in the dialogue of Alfred Hitchcock's *Notorious*.

Expressive air-pockets of dead silence. They are theatrical, and relatively easy to manage on film or on stage (think of Pinter). But how does anyone get them into fiction, where the flow of words must continue line by line, page by page, until the whole thing stops?

We often think of silence as being a blank, a null set, or of all silences being similar, expressing the same thing, the same nothing. We may not actually need John Cage, however, to show us that silence is an intensifier—that it strengthens whatever stands on either side of it. Directed in this way, silence takes on a different emotion, a different color, for whatever it flows through or flows between.

What's remarkable is the degree to which Americans have distrusted silence and its parent condition, stillness. In this country, silence is often associated with madness, mooncalfing, woolgathering, laziness, hostility, and stupidity. Stillness is regularly associated with death. The distrust of silence and stillness comes to us as a form of muddleheaded late-Puritanism, which looks upon idle hands as the devil's playground, and silence, like Hester Prynne's silence, as privatized rebellion, a refusal to join the team.

The daydreaming child, or daydreaming adult, is usually an object of contempt or therapy. Vitality in our culture, by contrast, has everything to do with speed and talk. In postmodernism, speed and information, combined through data processing, have moved into cyberspace. It is no wonder that the metaphor of the superhighway has stuck and has become an instant inter-national cliché. But when speed is made to be the defining fea-ture of action, violence is usually not far away, violence defined here as the loss of control under conditions of great velocity. Violence, unlike daydreaming, is not—this is worth our atten-tion—an object of contempt. Fear, perhaps, but not contempt.

Our fascination with violence is equal to our fascination with data processing; they are two coins in the same pocket.

◆

WHAT CONCEIVABLE RELATION is there between narrative violence and data processing? Speed, for one thing, and the necessity of coping with information that may be both dangerous and evanescent. People who work all day at com-puters often get keyed up, tense, and anxious because of the speed of the information flow. It does not seem to me that a day spent reading from pages has the same effect because the information flows at a different rate. On computers, infor-mation seems to move at great speed because users sit still in front of a screen. In this century, we have all learned to sit still in front of screens: movie and TV screens, computer screens, windshield/windscreens. As we sit still in front of these screens, we often witness representations of great violence. Stillness on one side, violence or speed on the other. People who can't sit still in front of these screens are said to have another twentieth-century invention, an affliction called attention deficit disorder.

◆

VELOCITY UNDERSTOOD IN relation to action and language has been, throughout this century, one of those ideo-logical headaches that will not go away. The peculiar and im-measurable speed of language as it carries information is a special problem of the twentieth century, because we are being bombarded by information at a rate unknown to previous eras, information produced by the forces of industrialization and urbanization, and the mass production of commodities and populations. The resulting data-nausea and information sick-ness are probably unique, at least on a mass scale, to our time.

Information sickness has lately become a concern for anyone who aspires to write fiction. Fiction involves a conversion: a conversion of information into experience. In the early part of this century, the critic Walter Benjamin worried over the displacement of experience by information: Excessive quantities of information in daily life, he thought, would block the experience of being transported by the storyteller. When that happens, the reader or the listener gets stuck at the level of data. Everything becomes discursive, with no sense of what Gertrude Stein later called "the excitement of contemporariness," the transformation of information into the experience of story.

◆

WITH HER CUSTOMARY goofy and cryptic insight, Gertrude Stein noticed that something was happening to the experience of time in the reading of fiction after the turn of the century. In her essay "How Writing Is Written," published in 1935, she observes that in the twentieth century, events "have lost their interest for people." Events, she says, have become like syrup.

This is a curious idea. It suggests that action, in fiction, has been drained of some intrinsic interest. We still need action, of course, but when we have it in front of us we don't notice it as much as readers did in previous centuries. In this sense, action is like the syrup just referred to, or a drug. If you are a cigarette smoker, you know what it is like to need a cigarette when you don't have one, yet not even notice when you light up and actually begin smoking. The craving is often sharper than the satisfaction. Action, as Gertrude Stein understood, has turned into just this kind of narcotic. You don't get interested in a narcotic; you just need it. Needing something is not the same thing as being interested in the thing itself.

This is an idea at the center of certain forms of modernism. There is a branch of modernism that distrusts all things in motion and trusts all things that are still. Gertrude Stein said that soldiers standing around on street corners during and after World War I, doing nothing much, were more interesting to people than when the soldiers went over the top. Although she does not say so in her essay, and certainly would not have said so, *A Farewell to Arms*—which is after all a love story with World War I somewhere there in the background—continues to be read when novels about trench warfare have disappeared.

This idea, that events have become like a syrup, may be incorrect. But what if you substitute the phrase "violent events" for "events"? What if violence itself is the syrup of our time, a syrup that we are not actually interested in but still need?

Gertrude Stein went on to praise herself, James Joyce, and Proust for writing fiction in which "nothing much happens." "For our purposes," she says, "events have no importance."

◆

THIS CLAIM, THAT events have no importance, is interesting to me because of its remarkable and stubborn absurdity. To find events unimportant is to imagine oneself shielded from the terrors of history. During World War II, Gertrude Stein was not always shielded—she was at times deeply frightened—and after that war she was once again interested in events.

Mixed with her silliness, however, are ideas and statements that, once heard, do not go away. "And so what I am trying to make you understand," she wrote, "is that every contemporary writer has to find out what is the inner time-sense of his contemporariness."

◆

"THE INNER TIME-SENSE of his contemporariness"— what is this? And what if the inner time-sense of our era has something to do with stillness, stillness through which action flows, stillness that has a quality of excitement to it, stillness that has not been dulled by narcosis and information sickness? To answer this question, we might begin with a novel from 1884—a novel saturated with American violence.

> Two or three days and nights went by; I reckon I might
> say they swum by, they slid along so quiet and smooth
> and lovely. Here is the way we put in the time . . . we
> slid into the river and had a swim, so as to freshen up
> and cool off; then we set down on the sandy bottom

where the water was about knee deep, and watched
the daylight come. Not a sound, anywheres—perfectly
still—just like the whole world was asleep, only sometimes the bull-frogs a-cluttering, maybe.

Huck Finn follows this observation with a nineteen-line
sentence, a sentence of over three hundred words that I won't
quote here but which is worth looking up, something of a rhap-
sody, the longest sentence in his book, and, I think, one of the
most beautiful sentences in American literature. Near the beginning of chapter 19 of *Adventures of Huckleberry Finn,* the sentence
is therefore in close proximity to the death, by gunshot, of Huck's
friend Buck Grangerford in chapter 18, and the death, also by
gunshot, of Boggs, killed by Colonel Sherburn, in chapter 21.

It is as if Americans typically have their moments of stillness when those moments are framed on both sides by violence.
It is a peculiarly American form of Zen enlightenment, when
stillness can justify itself only by planting itself amid uproar.

◆

STILLNESS IN FICTION arises when the dramatic action pauses, and when the forward movement of thought appears to cease as well. Instead of the forward dramatic line we
(at least temporarily) have the absorption of the character into
the minutiae of the setting. The dynamics of desire and fear are
momentarily displaced by a rapt attention to small details, to
the cultivation of a moment's mood for its own sake without
any nervous straining after insight. Stillness is not the same as
an epiphany. Attention flows away from what is supposed to
command it toward the peripheries: the river, the bank, the
trash floating down the river, the sound of the cricket. In a
moment of stillness, the atmosphere supplants the action.

In these moments, the setting may take on the burden of
the feeling.

Any such moment is fascinating because, in most Western
literature, it simply cannot last. Threatened by desire, cravings,
and appetites of every variety, and by the onset of boredom, it
has a kind of otherworldliness. For this reason, stillness has its
sinister side: one of Burroughs's junkies staring for hours at his

Florsheim shoe; or Andy Warhol's impenetrable presentation of a self-contained blank-faced narcissism; or Norman Bates, at the conclusion of *Psycho,* wrapped in his blanket, sitting immobilized in a room as blank as he is.

We might say about these forms of stillness that they have been traumatically fixated, unable to enlarge themselves or to develop. One's freedom in such instances, contaminated by an overpowering fear of shame or death, is the freedom not to make a move, any move. One becomes a junkie, or an artist, or a murderer, in order to enlarge one's capacities not to move, or to be moved.

◆

IN CONTEMPORARY GOTHIC mainstream literature, stillness at times has been shunted, or wrenched, away from pleasure and quietism, toward something that imitates the postures of death in an effort to fool it and to keep it safely at a distance. If you play dead, in these works, you won't die. One feels the presence of this kind of traumatized camouflage in several of Burroughs's novels, but also in the works of Kathy Acker, Bret Easton Ellis, Mary Gaitskill, and, in Europe, Botho Strauss and Ian McEwen. The landscape of contemporary fiction is full of this kind of camouflage, a sort of zombie dandyism.

My own interest in stillness has more to do with its benign features and with the great difficulty we have in expressing them. Because stillness lies toward the extremes of both the pleasure principle and the death instinct, it is often associated—perhaps unfortunately—with drugged blankness or morbidity. Boredom or deathliness keeps trying to appropriate it. Imagine a person who stays on the phone with a lover, in a state of silent mutual happiness. To a third party this silence would probably give the wrong impression—that is, silence and stillness are always open to misinterpretation. From a distance ecstasy often looks a bit overdetermined.

◆

"BE STILL," WE say, usually to children. Learn to be quiet and settled. Or we say, "It's still here." It has survived something. In both these usages, the word is associated with peaceful endurance or calm. The state of calm can be dynamic. Charles Ives claimed that his music was meant to expose "a kind of furious calm."

◆

I AM HAVING coffee with a friend. I tell her I am writing about stillness and ask her what books come to mind when I mention the subject. Virginia Woolf, she says, in *The Waves,* and Michael Ondaatje's writing generally, but *The English Patient* in particular. I myself have thought of Woolf, the dying away of the wind in the last section of *To the Lighthouse.* Or Proust: the opening pages of *Swann's Way* and the closing pages of *Time Regained*.

Another friend nods when I mention stillness. "Oh, right," he says. "The sections between the murders in *Pulp Fiction*. People sitting around and talking about nothing much, before they start shooting." Without meaning to, I agree with him. I forget to ask him if he means shooting a gun, or shooting up. It is not the shootings and murders in *Pulp Fiction* that interest people, but the sections in between, the sections full of talk. Nevertheless, the violence is necessary in order to make the stillness possible, as in Huck Finn. Violence frames it. For this reason, Tarantino's movie feels, much of the time, like a comedy or something with a joke structure. It is one instance of Gertrude Stein's claims about events: No one is interested in the violence in *Pulp Fiction,* but it is needed, like a narcotic fix, so that the rest of the story may go on.

◆

BENIGN STILLNESS IS simply one of the hardest psychic conditions to get on paper, and when the effort fails, as it usually does, the result looks like bad prose poetry or aggressively oversensitive rhetoric. One has to struggle against the narrative necessities of fiction in order to get a moment of stillness into the story in the first place, and in this struggle, the tendency is to lurch toward overstatement, out of a fear of boring the reader. But there is boredom and boredom. The composer Erik Satie claimed that boredom was "mysterious and profound." All the same, few literary tonalities sound worse than an overstated and overdescribed hush, full of insufferable displays of bejeweled feelings.

It's just possible that benign stillness has become a condition in our time that everyone feels now and then but that almost no one can describe with much accuracy. This has everything to do with what adult readers will believe and accept about their own past experiences. My sense of these matters is that we have become remarkably fluent in our narratives in describing violence and complaint but timid and insecure in describing moments of repose. In the nineteenth century, the reverse was true. Chekhov, for example, writes absolutely convincing scenes of stasis, but he rushes through moments of violence, such as the child-murder scene in his story "In the Ravine," as if such violence were quite unbelievable.

The power of stillness: an intensifier, a marker, an ability to define what surrounds it, using antidramatic, antinarrative means. What all stories want to get to, but cannot for the most part include.

But the issue is even more basic than that, more personal. I like to imagine that stillness can be made worthy of our attention. If stillness can be given different shadings—erotic, sorrowful, even terse or endangered—then there is cause for hope in several directions at once. Think of how Chekhov, or for that matter Satie, made the condition of boredom endlessly dynamic.

If, however, we have truly lost the ability to be interested in stillness, in the intricacies of psychic motionlessness, then we will have lost the capacity to be accurate about an entire dimension of our experiences.

◆

THREE EXAMPLES.

The Great Gatsby is so much a part of our national mythology and our required reading lists that its writerly oddities tend to be overlooked in the rush to get the book "prepared," and term papers written. In this novel and in *Tender Is the Night,* Fitzgerald regularly stops his scenes with a peculiar brilliance that's easy to miss. In *Gatsby* these tricks of timing are a sign of the narrator's, Nick Carraway's, habit of removing his perceptions from the scene in which he is participating, partly because he is dazzled, and partly because he is also suspicious of bedazzlement and emotional fraud. At times the stillness effect seems intended to evoke romantic longing. In all cases it sparks a characteristic feeling of odd wonder, a poisonously pleasant emotion in the presence of the wealth that the book is at pains to diagnose and to treat.

The first chapter is thick with such moments. Nick has arrived at the Buchanans'. "The windows were ajar and gleaming white against the fresh grass outside that seemed to grow a little way into the house." This is a very odd sentence. It's surprising that it got past the Scribner copyeditors. Infused with the kind of bland surrealism you feel when you stare for too long at a Hopper painting, this moment is immediately followed by the famous paragraph in which Jordan and Daisy are introduced, seemingly airborne, both of them sitting on a sofa. As dazzling as they are, Nick is fixed on the peripheries. "I must have stood," he writes, "for a few moments listening to the whip and snap of the curtains and the groan of a picture on the wall."

Those few moments count for everything in this scene. They comprise a piece of time in which Nick's consciousness has almost stopped. As a narrator, Nick will not be rushed. The whip and the groan tell us that this is a haunted house, that the objects in it are complaining and halfway sentient, and they warn us, in a sort of elegant comic gothic style, that all is not well at the Buchanans'. In the following sentence, Tom shuts the door and "the caught wind died out about the room, and the curtain and the rugs and the two young women ballooned slowly to the floor." Notice how Tom has the ability to catch the wind and to kill it. Notice how, in this moment of stillness, Tom pulls the women earthward, how they descend to his level.

Fitzgerald was seldom afraid of literalizing his metaphors. This gives his writing its characteristic cavalier glossiness and, as he moved toward the composition of *Tender Is the Night,* its progressive structural waywardness. In *Gatsby,* rugs and beautiful women could balloon to the floor because he believed, with a touching faithfulness, that most readers could share his vision and understand the figures for it. In his fiction there's a kind of manic exhilaration in encountering beautiful objects, an exhilaration habitually deflated by a single brutal gesture. The puncturing of these balloons, the way things drift earthward, the brutality behind the glare of riches—all these shattered displays give *Gatsby* a curious rhythm. Stillness—a rapt gaze—alternates with violence, very much in the American style. When I close my eyes and imagine the book, I see its characters either standing immobilized, watching and waiting, or engaged in orgies or automotive manslaughter or homicide. I cannot see anything between these two poles.

◆

SECOND EXAMPLE.

In chapter 8 of Marilynne Robinson's *Housekeeping,* Sylvie takes Ruth, her niece, to her "secret place," up the lake from Fingerbone, to a site of abandoned homesteads. Sylvie has promised Ruth that children, or the spirits of children—she is characteristically vague on this point—may meet them there. But when they arrive on the spot, Sylvie abandons Ruth. Ruth goes into the cellar of a ruined, collapsed house, the remnant of a homestead, where she pulls out loose planks until she is sweating. She realizes that there are no spirit children there: "They were light and spare and thoroughly used to the cold, and it was almost a joke to them to be cast out into the woods, even if their eyes were gone and their feet were broken." Having thought this, Ruth sits down and waits for Sylvie to return.

The following passage is immune to quotation. It cannot be successfully excerpted. Its mixture of grieving and rapture seems to me to avoid the florid baroque in which some writers might have indulged. Marilynne Robinson, and Ruth, her narrator, quite possibly find stillness more interesting than action, with the result that the rhetoric does not need to be cranked up. In any case, in this section, Ruth is letting stillness inhabit her, allowing the chill to take her over, the literal chill and the metaphysical chill of Sylvie's abandonment of her. It's a moment of vision, and it is rapturous. Once Ruth has absorbed the cold, and absorbed the fact that the spirits will not return to her, Sylvie comes back, wraps Ruth in her overcoat, and rocks her. Then she takes her home across the water.

This section, like much of *Housekeeping,* feels deeply ritualistic to me. In it, gloom and wonder start to shift positions; Ruth's condition as a child, and Sylvie's status as an adult, never clear anywhere in the novel, are collapsed and pulled apart again. This section of the book seems to be fixated on the ground under Ruth, but the book insists that the ground on which one stands is a material illusion anyway, as is the first fundamental of that illusion, the house one lives in. Like Jay Gatsby, Sylvie seems to fall rather frequently into trance states. At first Ruth tries to pry her out of these states. Then she stops trying, and *Housekeeping* itself falls into the trance, into a condition of a prolonged and permanent hush.

Trances, spirits, stillness. It is tempting to say that these elements begin to come together in a condition of loss, that what we have been talking about all along is loss, that stillness and silence are collaborators in waiting, but waiting without knowing what we are waiting for, waiting without an object in view. This is one of the ways in which I understand the process of grieving. The ground underneath us becomes immaterial, and we wait in full knowledge that what we wait for will not appear. There can be a curious calm and alertness, an animal sensitivity, to this condition.

◆

ELSEWHERE, IN AN essay on the American West, Marilynne Robinson has argued that our mythologies about the West are warped in the direction of gunplay, warfare and conquest, John Wayne, open spaces, and slaughter. What if, she suggests, alongside that noisy male-dominated set of myths, there is another one more commonly perceived by women, a West dominated by space and silence? A West of silences, in which the openness is an invitation not to action, but to what I have been calling here a trance condition?

Perhaps all along I have been talking about the Midwest, my home territory, and my persistent amazement about it.

◆

THIRD AND LAST set of examples: Wright Morris, *The Works of Love,* an American novel from 1952, and *Fire Sermon,* from 1971.

The Works of Love, about a man whose life never amounts to very much and who lives his life in a semitrance, is written in a relentlessly peculiar style. Things and people suddenly appear and vanish in it. Whole paragraphs are given over to digressions. After a few awkward gestures toward plot, the novel's story line, such as it is, renounces conflict in favor of meditation. Declarative sentences often switch direction and conclude with question marks. Even the efforts at characterization are halfhearted: The women in the novel are only half seen, if that, and often at a disadvantage. Transitions are abrupt, occasionally baffling. Isolated moments are elongated for pages, while years flash by like a deck of cards shuffled by an impatient dealer. If it were not for its seemingly banal Midwestern settings and lower-middle-class characters and laconic narrative voice, the book would have been classified long ago as European experimentalism at its most willful and extreme.

And yet the book has a subject, a clear one, and a clear means of addressing it. *The Works of Love* is about a man who wants to love but who in his bewilderment does not know how to go about it. Some element, common to others, is missing in his character. In most respects he is bewildered and stays that way all his life. In virtually all matters, he does not have a clue. Wright Morris has no interest in turning this situation into one that is meant to charm and seduce, *à la* Forrest Gump. His protagonist, Will Brady, draws a blank no matter where he is. He is not especially lovable, and the narrative keeps him at a distance. The result is a terribly eerie novel about a specific kind of American emptiness, an emptiness filled with things and pragmatism and people. Will Brady lives in a state of constant distraction. Having grown up on the Great Plains, he is infected with emptiness and takes it with him everywhere. "This desolate place [Morris writes], this rim of the world, had been God's country to Adam Brady, but to Caroline Clayton, a godforsaken hole. Perhaps only Will Brady could combine these two points of view. He could leave it, that is, but he could never get over it."

Which is to say that emptiness and the sacred are combined for him. If *Gatsby* has sentences of stillness, and *Housekeeping* long passages of it, then *The Works of Love* is an experiment of sorts in writing a novel with a central character who is still all the way through.

The lyrical emptiness of Will Brady's circumstances is conveyed, not in the European style through lavish attention to the vacancy of thought rising through higher and higher forms of abstraction, but through a careful attention to hotel lobbies, city parks, and railroad stations. In America every emotion, even emptiness, is supported by American things; our pragmatism seems to insist on this. The novel—I am not the first to make this observation about Wright Morris's fiction—feels like a succession of photographs. The photographs are taken with detachment but are lovingly assembled. The effect, however, is to reduce to nothing the dynamics of the action and to increase to absolute proportions the attention to things at rest. The effect is transfixing, very rich, and deeply disturbing.

With its constant shift of perspectives combined with its subject, the novel starts to feel like Grant Wood's *American Gothic* as repainted by Braque, as a cubist collage. The reader feels a bit stunned, as Will Brady does, at sea in an ocean of detail. The eye cannot find the proper object of its desire anywhere. It does not even know where to look, in this abundance of persistent muted objects. Desire gets lost, in this bland midwestern Zen, even on Will Brady's wedding day. Here, for example, is a paragraph in which he forgets to look at his wife during the ceremony (he is looking through a doorway instead and, as usual, is transfixed):

> They were married in Bruno, a Bohemian town in
> the rolling country just south of the Platte, four or five
> miles' drive from where her father had a big farm. They
> were married in the church where Ralph Bassett had
> married her. It sat on the rise, overlooking the town, and
> as it was June the door stood open and Will Brady could

see the buggies drawn up beneath the shade trees out in front. An elderly man was combing sandburs from a dark mare's tail. It was quiet on the rise, without a leaf stirring, but in the sunny hollow along the tracks a westerly breeze was turning the wheel of a giant windmill. It looked softly blurred, quite a bit the way the heat made everything look in Indian Bow, with the air, like a clear stream of water, flowing up from the hot earth. Near the windmill a man was sinking a post, and the sound of the blows, like jug corks popping, came up in the pause that his mallet hung in the air. Fred Blake had to remind him—nudging him sharply—to kiss the bride.

This is thickly lyrical but it would be a mistake to call it heartwarming. The narrative, taking Will Brady's side of things, collaborates with him by somehow not noticing his wife. She is dramatically at the center of this scene, but the drama has been pushed to the periphery, and the peripheries (the windmill, the mallet) have been nudged to the center, in the interest of stillness. I think Morris wants to convey a feeling of loneliness and distraction at the center of action here, but I don't think "alienation" is the right word for that feeling. It can hit any of us when we are not quite inside the action we are performing, and it is intensified, for example at parties or other social gatherings, when we are supposed to be feeling emotions that we may not have—when public displays of sentiment are called for—but acting seems out of the question.

Many readers, baffled or frustrated by the gruff, dry displacement of drama in Morris's fiction, may give up on it before the love for places and things becomes evident. Like the otherwise dissimilar Willa Cather and Jack Kerouac, Morris is often in an elegiac mode, writing about, to use one of his favorite phrases from Samuel Beckett, "things about to disappear." As a photographer, Morris has shown himself to be transfixed—that word again—by objects, both human and inanimate, that have sustained much use. They have been weathered, and in his photographs and his fiction they possess a gaunt, stark geometry.

The Works of Love details dispassionately Will Brady's failure as a chicken farmer (his hens die) and as a home builder (he neglects to install a furnace in his basement), and as a father and husband, but in a sense the novel has been waiting all along for Will Brady to get old, for his baffled heartiness to spin upon a still point—a park bench or a rented room. Late in the novel, living in a rooming house, Will Brady finds himself once again alone, and in the evenings he walks down toward Lincoln Park. This situation provokes the narrative into an extraordinary tightlipped grandeur:

> If there was a moon, or a cool breeze off the lake, Will Brady would walk through the park to the water, where he would stroll along the pilings, or under the trees on the cinder bridle path. He had walked on cinders, he seemed to remember, somewhere before. As he had in the past, he would have to sit down and tap them out of his shoes. In the dusk there would be lights on in the Wrigley tower, an air-plane beacon would sweep the sky, and at Oak Street beach people would be lying in the warm sand. The drinking fountain would give off a strong chlorine smell. He would wet his face at the fountain, then take his seat among those people who had come to the beach but didn't care to take off their clothes; who had been hot in their rooms, and perhaps lonely in their minds. In the dark they could speak what they had on their minds without troubling about their faces, the sound of their voices, or who their neighbor was. Will Brady was their neighbor. He sat with his coat folded in his lap, his shirtsleeves rolled.

That's beautiful. It goes on for another three pages. It moves somewhere between detachment, placidity, and the inevitability of sadness. Will Brady's story has been subsumed here into a Chicago nocturne. The story, such as it is, can wait.

In another one of his novels, *Fire Sermon,* Wright Morris follows a boy and his aged Uncle Floyd as they break into the house of Floyd's sister, empty of her, but still filled with her things.

The boy said, "Aren't there any lights?" and looked for the switch on the wall. There was no switch, but on the table at the bedside stood a lamp, with a green shade, a wick curled in the bowl of clear oil. Uncle Floyd *kicked the door, opening it wider, then stomped in to throw up the blind at the window opening out on the porch. That did little good because it was blocked by the iceboxes. The room smelled of burned lamp wick, coal oil, and the odor the boy associated with his mother's clothes closet, at once sweet and* sour. On the floor was a saucer of soured milk, the edges nibbled by mice. A shoebox full of postcard pictures of cats, kittens, and puppies, along with postcards and let-ters, sat on the shelf below the lamp. The boy recognized the last letter, with the Smokey the Bear stamp, as his own. On the table at the foot of the bed, where they could be reached through the iron frame, soiled towels and dishcloths were piled in a washbowl, held down by a plate dirty with food smears. At the side a comb is stuck into the bristles of a brush with a silver back, and a small oval picture in a frame stamped with colored flow-ers. The picture showed a bearded man, seated erect on a chair, with a child on his knee holding a bird cage. The boy moved closer to see if the cage held a bird, but it is empty and the door is open. A woman stands behind him, one white hand resting on his shoulder, her hair parted and gathered in a bun at the neck.

This rhapsodic inventory—the things Aunt Viola carried—is wonderfully unstable. It cannot stay in the past tense and shifts uneasily into the present. The woman in the photograph comes out of the photograph, and, through a trick of faulty reference, puts her hand on the boy's shoulder. The descrip-tion of Aunt Viola's house goes on for several more pages, and eventually the inventory includes the boy's uncle.

"Uncle Floyd," the boy said, but remained standing in the door. The green blind softened the light, and with nothing in the room to block it or absorb it the boy felt its presence. Within it, captive, he saw the figure seated

on the narrow-backed armless rocker, both the seat
and the back covered with pads made of patchwork
quilting. Two dozen patches on the back side alone, in
all shapes, colors, and materials. Everything left over
had been put into it, as into this house. The old man
who sat there did not impress the boy as his own great-
uncle, Floyd Warner, but another object preserved from
the past. Perhaps this corner room had been reserved
for objects of that sort. . . . The boy really knew nothing about such matters and perhaps that proved to his
advantage. He brought so little to what he saw, he saw
what was there.

This reminds me of Kerouac, but Kerouac after detox, and
it is very close to the emotion of entranced waiting we find in
Housekeeping. Speculation—in both senses of that word—
is at work here. This kind of writing takes nerve and confidence to do, to assume that the reader will adapt to this vision and will be patient enough to wait for the next action,
when it eventually comes. The style does not share Fitzgerald's
Princetonian confidence that the metaphorical visions will
be magically conveyed to the reader. It's too dour for that.
Stillness has fully inhabited this narrative voice; like the prose
writing of Samuel Beckett, a stoic lyric intelligence seems to be
aware of the reader but eager to keep some distance from that
reader. In order to create its atmosphere, the excitement of its
contemporariness, it must slow down, rather than speed up, and
turn its back slightly to us.

The purpose of this slowdown is to locate a sense of wonder squarely at the center of the story. Wright Morris's intelligence is such that he constantly withdraws from the scene of his
own story in order to express his wonder at it, and, in a sense,
his detachment from it. It takes nerve to keep the action moving, but it takes more nerve to slow it down or to stop it, and a
particular kind of courage to keep what seems to be peripheral
at the center. Morris's fiction—like Charles Reznikoff's and Lorine Niedecker's poetry—has this nerve and eccentricity as its
trademark, mostly, I think, at the service of wonder.

Morris is quite explicit about this. In the last chapter of *Fire Sermon* the boy finds a coin "in the pocket of a coat, draped on a doornail, that had survived all the people who had spent or saved it since 1879. The meaning of this escaped him in a manner he found satisfying. Already he was old enough to gaze in wonder at life." Wonderment never quite gets used to whatever it is looking at.

So finally we arrive at wonder, which, for me, is at the bottom level, the ground floor, of stillness. Wonder is at the opposite pole of worldliness, just as stillness is at the opposite pole from worldly action. Wonder puts aside the known and accepted, along with sophistication, and instead serves up an intelligent naïveté. Why should anything be as it is? Why are things as they are? What if some fiction thrives, not on statements and claims, but on questions? Wonder is about the last emotion one would expect to find in contemporary America, and that gives it a power to dramatize the excitement of contemporariness, with meanings that will escape us in a manner we will all find satisfying.

Notes

Walter Benjamin, "The Storyteller," in *Illuminations,* edited by Hannah Arendt, translated by Harry Zohn (New York: Schocken Books, 1969), 83–110.

Gertrude Stein, "How Writing Is Written," in *How Writing Is Written,* edited by Robert Bartlett Haas (Los Angeles: Black Sparrow Press, 1974), 151–60.

DAVID KIRBY is the Robert O. Lawton Distinguished Professor of English at Florida State University and lives in Tallahassee, Florida. Among his thirty books is *The House on Boulevard St.: New and Selected Poems,* which was a finalist for the 2007 National Book Award. He has also written on music for the *Chicago Tribune,* the *Christian Science Monitor,* the *New York Times Book Review, TriQuarterly,* the *Washington Post,* the *South Florida Sun-Sentinel, Georgia Music,* and others, and his latest book is *Little Richard: The Birth of Rock 'n' Roll.*

Kirby was a featured writer at the 2009 Ohio University Spring Literary Festival.

![black bar]

Thirteen Things I
Hate about Poetry

DAVID KIRBY

![black bar]

*YOU WROTE THIS ESSAY FOR
me, reader—thanks!* What I'm going to present to you is a series of questions or propositions about poetry offered to me
over the years. We begin a few years ago when a professor
from one of the sciences greets me by saying that it must be
nice to be in a field where one can "just make things up."
And out of my meditation on that statement and others like
it arises a profound paradox. Or two, actually. The first is
that poetry is both the most worthless and the most highly
valued commodity in the world. And the second paradox
rises from the first; it is that everyone hates poetry and everyone is a poet.

Each of the thirteen parts of this essay begins with a verbatim comment about poetry made to me by someone on
my campus. I've conflated all my interlocutors into a single
speaker I'll call "Q," based on the scientist who buttonholed me
originally. "Q" denotes "Question" but may also remind you

of the irascible know-it-all in the James Bond films who says "Pay attention, 007!" as he gives the agent his gadgets.

With minimal editing, every statement you are about to read is a verbatim comment about poetry made to me by someone on this campus. All hems and haws are edited out, and I do confess to a certain embroidery when it comes to my replies. You'll also notice that my persona in this paper is able to quote reams of material; with the exception of a few limericks I probably shouldn't include, I've never had that enviable quality of being able to memorize at length, so I can guarantee you that those parts of my replies were gotten from books. There's a certain amount of repetition, but that's because some propositions were put to me more than once. And if I tend to give myself the last word, remember: words are all I have.

I

Q: David, it must be nice to just make things up.

A: Well, I do make things up. But I don't "just" make things up. Besides, at times, it seems my work would go a whole lot faster if I had something external to examine: a quark or isotope or potsherd.

Q: See, that's what we do in my field: we look at the argument and the evidence that backs it up. So it's a little difficult for me to judge a poem, since poets deal in emotions.

A: Actually, we poets use evidence, although we call it "images." And we make arguments, though we call them "poems."

Q: Well, "images"! I mean, that's just your imagination, right?

A: Yes and no. The Neoplatonic philosopher Iamblichus says that "things more excellent than every image are expressed through images." And in his essay "The Poet," Emerson speaks of the universal appeal of images: "Some stars, lilies, leopards, a crescent, a lion, an eagle, or other figure which came into credit God knows how, on an old rag of bunting, blowing in the wind on a fort at the ends of the earth, shall make the blood tingle under the rudest or the most conventional exterior." His point? "The people fancy they hate poetry, and they are all poets and mystics!"

II

Q: Well, I guess I just don't get poetry.

A: But do you get Rossini's *String Quartet in C Major?* Or if you're at a dance recital, do you stand up right there in row H and shout, "Stop! I don't get it!"?

Q: Yeah, but even when I get a poem, it doesn't always mean I like it.

A: Well, you don't have to. A few years ago, Barbara and I were at this dinner party, and one of your colleagues in the sciences kept wanting to know how I wrote poetry and how I knew if it was good or not, and I said, "Well, experience helps a lot," and she said if experience was all there was to it, then we could find a cure for cancer tomorrow, and I said I didn't say experience was all there was to it, just that it helped a lot, and that as far as knowing whether a poem was good or not, it was good if an editor accepted it, so she wanted to know how the editor knew if it was good or not in an objective, i.e., quantifiable sense, and I'm doing my best to stay polite, but just then her scientist husband joins her, and the two of them begin to raise their voices, and even though I haven't said anything about all the dumb science that's out there as well as the faked science, not to mention the evil science, suddenly they're mad at me, or maybe they're really mad at poetry.

I don't blame them, I guess. Sometimes I get mad at poetry myself.

III

Q: Hey, David, I've been meaning to ask you: how long does it take you to write a poem?

A: Well, sometimes a couple of years.

Q: A couple of years! To write a page and a half?

A: A couple of years to decide exactly what I want to say. Then maybe half an hour or so to put it down on paper.

Q: Half an hour—that's more like it.

A: Yes and no, because the immediate time factor's not all that important. In 1877, John Ruskin published an essay about Whistler's paintings in which he said, "I have seen, and heard, much of cockney impudence before now; but never expected to hear a coxcomb ask two hundred guineas for flinging a pot of paint in the public's face." Whistler sued, and in the course of the trial, he was applauded when Ruskin's attorney questioned him about perhaps his boldest painting, "Nocturne in Black and Gold: The Falling Rocket," and asked the painter if he thought it fair to receive 200 guineas for the two days it took him to complete the work. "No," Whistler replied dramatically, "I ask it for the knowledge of a lifetime." Whistler won the case, incidentally.

Q: So even he was saying it only takes an artist a few hours to turn something out.

A: Well, then a couple more years to revise it.

Q: You revise your stuff?

A: I do!

Q: But doesn't that spoil the freshness of your writing?

A: The writing has to *appear* fresh, not *be* fresh. And usually it takes a lot of work with hammer and tongs and bellows to give that appearance of freshness. Besides, sometimes an editor *makes* me revise.

Q: You mean—you mean you let somebody *change* your poem?!?

A: Well, they're publishing it, so why shouldn't they offer their suggestions? Besides, nine out of ten suggestions make the poem better. Okay, make that seven out of ten.

Q: Still! You're the poet. I mean, you wrote the poem; why change it?

A: You know, I think it all comes down to what you mean by the verb "to write." The English poet and critic James Fenton said that "the writing of a poem is like a child throwing stones into a mineshaft. You compose first, then you listen for the reverberation." You have to hear the sound before you can decide what you want to do with all those reverberations.

Q: Okay, that would make sense in my field, where we have to adjust our expectations as new data comes in. But you're writing for yourself.

A: Yes and no. All poetry begins as self-expression. But if I only write for myself, who's going to want to read what I've written except me? I tell my students that, at some point, writing stops being self-expression and starts being communication, or it fails. Whether you read me or not, I'm writing for you.

IV

Q: David, my kids listen to rap all the time. Is rap poetry?
A: No.

V

Q: David, are the songs of Bob Dylan poetry?

A: No. A poem is made of words. A pop song is made of words, instrumental music, and percussion. Especially percussion: the first two pages of the Tallahassee phone directory would make a pretty good pop song if you set it to the right beat.

If you've ever played an instrument, you know how hard it is to play a single line of music, much less compose entire works. But at the Rock and Roll Hall of Fame in Cleveland, you see a lot of lyrics that the artists wrote on hotel stationery and napkins, because words are the least important of the three elements that make up a song. But in poetry, words are the only element.

Let's go back to rap for a second. In music, as in poetry, when a tradition begins to get stale, usually a vigorous countertradition comes along to shake things up. Ever heard of John Skelton? Like other formal poets, he used elaborate patterns in his verse but then began to feel that they didn't really convey the sound of spoken English. So he continued to use rhymes, but he rhymed certain words only as long as he wanted to, and then he'd begin a new rhyme. And he used very short lines, maybe three to six words long. So Skeltonic verse, as it came to be called, sounds like this:

> . . . if he speak plain,
> Then he lacketh brain,
> He is but a fool;
> Let him go to school,
> On a three-footed stool
> . . . .
> And if ye stand in doubt
> Who brought this rhyme about,
> *My name is Colin Clout.*

That's from "Colin Clout," the author of which lived circa 1460–1529. John Skelton: the world's first rapper.

VI

Q: Okay, now you brought up this whole thing about form. The way I see it, the only real poetry is formal poetry; otherwise, the poet's just making things up. I think the people who write free verse are just too lazy to put in all that technical stuff.

A: Gee, I'll have to pass that on to those big do-nothings Walt Whitman, T. S. Eliot, Ezra Pound, William Carlos Williams, Wallace Stevens, Marianne Moore, Elizabeth Bishop, Gwendolyn Brooks, Robert Lowell, Allen Ginsberg, Sharon Olds, Billy Collins, and the several thousand poets whose careers they've influenced, including pretty much everyone who has won the Nobel or Pulitzer Prize and is included in *The Norton Anthology of Modern Poetry.*

Q: Well, I guess I just don't get it. I wish poets still wrote the kind of poems I read when I was going to school.

A: They do. R. S. Gwynn, Marilyn Hacker, Andrew Hudgins, Sydney Lea, Marilyn Nelson, and Mary Jo Salter are only a few of the many poets who still use the old forms. Free verse just means there are two ways to write poetry, not one. Look, you might do particle physics, but if an apple falls out of a tree, it'll still hit you on the head as it would have in Newton's day, right?

I wrote once that a free-verse writer is like a kid on a river bank who's skipping stones across the water. Some of the stones the kid throws land just a few feet away and disappear immediately, while others splash a couple of times and sink. But some stones skip six, seven, eight times. Ping, ping, ping: farther and farther they go until they disappear in the darkness. The kid's a bit of a risk-taker, and some of the risks don't pay off, though it's worth it finally to make that one perfect toss and hear that one stone splash off into the distance, ever more faintly.

VII

Q: I really enjoyed those stories you write. I call them "stories" because they sound like stories to me, not poems.

A: Correct: they're narrative poems.

Q: So poems can tell stories? I didn't know that.

A: Then I have three words for you: Homer, Dante, Milton.

VIII

Q: David, I noticed that you use a lot of humor in your poems.

A: Oh, you caught me!

Q: I didn't know poetry could be funny.

A: Then I have three words for you—Chaucer, Shakespeare, Jonathan Swift . . .

Q: I mean, isn't most poetry about death or something?

A: . . . Byron, Browning, Emily Dickinson . . .

Q: You're not being serious, David.

A: I am! Poetry can have the logic of a syllogism, but it can also have the logic of a joke. The poet Howard Nemerov argues that a poem and a joke are pretty much the same thing. You either get the joke or you don't, says Nemerov. If everyone else gets the joke and you don't, you can't complain that the joke is "subjective" or that it doesn't make sense; after all, it made sense to everyone else. If you're smart, you'll smile politely; if you're not, you'll give out a forced laugh that everyone will recognize as fake. Should someone have to explain the joke to you, the difficulty will be cleared up, but it's too late—you can still laugh, but your laughter is likely to be a grim chuckle rather than the hearty peals of the others, because the *joke's* funny, but not its explanation. Of course, the poem isn't usually met with laughter, says Nemerov, but with silence, "or the acknowledgement that it is so, it is as it is: that the miracle has happened again."

IX

Q: Hmm. Well, all I can say is, it must be nice to just make things up.

A: Hey, you gotta do what you gotta do to pay the bills.

Q: Yeah, I've heard you guys in English don't make as much as we do.

A: Oh, I'm talking about my intellectual debts.

Q: "Intellectual . . ."? I thought you were a poet!

A: True. But as Emerson says, "A poet is no rattlebrain, saying what comes uppermost, and because he says everything, saying, at last, something good; but a heart in unison with his time and country." Like that? Here's more: "The greatest genius is the most indebted man," says Emerson. "A great man does not wake up on some fine morning and say, 'I am full of life, I will go to sea and find an Antarctic continent: to-day I will square the circle: I will ransack botany, and find a new food for man: I have a new architecture in mind: I foresee a new mechanic power'; no, but he finds himself in the river of thoughts and events, forced onward by the ideas and necessities of his contemporaries. He stands where all the eyes of men look one way, and their hands all point in the direction in which he should go."

Q: Okay, okay. But the point is that you don't get paid for your poetry other than what you make as a professor.

A: Not get paid? To the contrary! Why, I wrote a poem just yesterday and sold it this morning for more than one hundred and seventy-five thousand dollars!

Q: One hundred sev—oh, I can see I need to keep my eye on you, David! I guess you can always make money other ways, though. Maybe you can sue somebody, like that Whistler fellow.

A: If I do, I hope I have better luck. It's true that Whistler won, but the jury awarded him only a farthing in damages, and the judge refused costs. So Whistler had to pay for everything, and he was ruined. Ruskin, far from gloating, was appalled by what he saw as Whistler's moral victory. He resigned his professorship at Oxford because he felt his very right to be a critic had been denied by the British legal system. If you're trying to go broke, art's a pretty reliable way to do so.

Then again, there's money in all the arts. It's the wealth of the intellect and the spirit. People who question the value of poetry need to consider this: why have there always been poets? As far as that goes, why is there a poet laureate but not a novelist laureate or playwright laureate, not to mention a composer/painter/sculptor/filmmaker laureate? There's not a single physicist or psychologist or economist laureate in the world. Since the dawn of history, every culture has had poets; why do people read and write poetry if it isn't hugely rewarding to them? The answer is that, just as there are lots of different intelligences—verbal and quantitative, sure, but also spatial, musical, and so on—there are lots of different kinds of wealth, and money is just one of them.

Q: Well, you're very quick with an analogy, David, but what you're saying is that poetry is worthless—in real terms, I mean. Metaphorically, it's worth a bundle; in real terms, though, poetry's worth nothing.

A: Yes and no. How's this: in a marvelous book of essays called *In the Blue Pharmacy,* poet Marianne Boruch says that Elizabeth Bishop's poetry is driven by a "useless . . . wonder which fills us sometimes, before we even think about it, with a rare, self-forgetful joy." Isn't that enough? "Useless wonder": that sounds pretty useful to me.

Q: Okay, you need to make up your mind.

A: Remember what Emerson said, that people hate poetry, yet they're all poets? Here's another way to put it: in my experience, (1) everyone thinks poetry is crazy or weird, and (2) everyone writes poetry.

Q: I don't write poetry, David.

A: You used to, though. You might not remember it, but you did. Everybody writes poetry, and then they stop. Why did you stop? Was it to do science? You can do science and write poetry; there are plenty of scientist poets out there. Or you can do science now and write poetry later; just don't give up.

X

Q: I know you give a lot of readings, David. What's it like to stand up there and bare yourself?

A: It's easy, since it's not me. The person you see behind the microphone is the same as the one you're talking to right now. But the person in the poem isn't me, even though he may have the same name.

Q: Well, he sounds like you! You're sure it isn't you?

A: Yes and no. The difference in the two Davids is that the one in the poems is always well-dressed, always articulate, and so on. Poetry Dave is a whole lot more attractive than Reality Dave. The only problem is that, whereas Reality Dave is as honest as the day is long, you can't always trust Poetry Dave; as you say, he makes things up.

XI

Q: The thing about poetry is, I just don't get it.

A: Me, neither! Well, I don't get it if I don't work at it, at least a little bit. I read in *The New York Times* that if anyone considers Umberto Eco's work difficult, he receives it as a compliment. Readers want to be involved in an act of mutual seduction, says Eco: "Only publishers and television people believe that people crave easy experiences."

Another way to put it, as one of your colleagues said to me once, is that "if you know what you're doing, it isn't research." Or this: the cubist Georges Braque said the only thing that counts in art is the thing you can't explain.

Q: That's okay for you, but couldn't you poets make it a little easier on us ordinary readers?

A: I'm not sure there's any such thing as an ordinary reader. Or that there should be. "We all get bored," says the young poet Roger Fanning in one of his poems, for "between mainstream culture (buy things) / and nature (in this case, rain), people tend to snooze," but then "poetry jolts awake the lucky few." Let poetry be for the lucky few, if that's how it is. We don't all have to do the same thing. I like poetry, but I like to take long walks with my wife. I like the movies.

XII

Q: In one of your poems, you refer to Sartre's *Being and Nothingness.* Now I know what that is, of course, but it seems to me you're writing for the elite few.

A: Well, sure! Why shouldn't the elite few experience exactly the same amount of pleasure as my hundreds of thousands of ordinary readers?

Q: But aren't you afraid you're going to lose your audience if you use too many arcane references, too many sesquipedalian words?

A: I don't think so. I'm going to presume my reader is pretty smart; I wouldn't insult him or her by presuming otherwise. The point is the whole world passes through art, and—maybe you've noticed—stuff that's incomprehensible and weird and offbeat is a big part of the world.

Marianne Boruch uses a wonderful analogy to suggest how poets work. As a telegraphist, Thomas Edison was supposed to be second to none, a fact he attributed to the deafness that allowed him to hear his instrument alone. Imagine the scene, says Boruch: "In that room, an island of quiet; then one imagines the beat from the incoming wire, two beats, three and four. Pauses held and let go, a meaningful rhythm. Bad news or good news, grief or love or both. So much like the making of a poem suddenly, the poet alert, waiting to translate something from somewhere, the whole terrible, private business."

In a word, the world taps on its key, and it's all those little dots and dashes—a wrecked car, a painted wooden albatross, a chant in a language we don't understand—that make up the poem. Presuming, of course, that the poet is as good a telegrapher as Edison.

XIII

Q: Aw, David, the thing about poetry is that I don't get it! Okay, so you're not just making things up. But if you're working at it so damned hard, can't you guys do better? Can't you write poems that are smart but don't go over the reader's head, that are funny but, not, you know, *just* funny, funny and substantial, too? Poems that are fresh and original yet well-crafted, that are demanding but don't require you to abandon everything else in your life and spend every waking hour reading some stupid poem? I want poems that tell stories, but not the way stories tell stories. I want the poem to look good on the page, to convey control, authority. But I also want poems that have that hands-in-pockets quality, as though the poet's a smart neighbor and I'm just talking to him and he's coming up with all this great stuff. And I want poems that tell you things you don't know or make you see things you haven't seen before, that provide new feelings, new ideas—poems that make you *feel ideas!* You poets use the "I" a lot. Who is that "I"? Is it you? It's okay if it's you, but I want it to be me, too! I want in! I want beauty! I want brains! I want a conversation. I want to talk to the old dead poets and the ones that are living right now and the ones that haven't been born yet, and I want it all on a page or a few pages, at most! That's what I want. That's the kind of poem I'm looking for. Can't you poets write poems like that?

A: I'm trying, brother. I'm trying.

CLAIRE BATEMAN'S books are *The Bicycle Slow Race, Friction, At the Funeral of the Ether, Clumsy, Leap,* and *Coronology and Other Poems.* The title poem from *Coronology* is also an e-chapbook of the same name produced by World Voices and available as a print chapbook from Serving House Press. She has received grants and fellowships from the National Endowment for the Arts, the Tennessee Arts Commission, the Surdna Foundation, and the New Millennium Poetry Prize. She lives in Greenville, South Carolina.

Bateman was a featured writer at the 2006 Ohio University Spring Literary Festival.

Some Questions about Questions

CLAIRE BATEMAN

THIS ESSAY WILL BE CHARACTERIZED by its lack of identifiable focus, internal transitions, and conclusion, for my goal is not to posit anything in particular, but rather to present my ongoing, ever-expanding web of personal speculation on the topic of questions in poetry.

Of course, you may legitimately see almost any poem as a question or a response to a question, though if you end up defining everything as a question, then nothing turns out to be a question—and it could be that in some metaparadoxical way, "nothing" *is* indeed a question—but what I want to talk about here is explicit, not implicit, questions in poetry; rhetorical formulations whose mailing address would be located somewhere in Bloom's taxonomy or its wider environs. And because the topic is one that tends to overflow any container into which one pours it, I'll also be exploring the idea of questions in other contexts—so please prepare for considerable thematic and definitional nebulosity.

◆

WHAT KIND OF *entity is a question?*

"O for a life of sensations, rather than thoughts," exclaimed Keats. Is a question a *thought* or a *sensation,* like that of itching, being tickled, or even burning?—after all, one may speak of "burning questions." While it has been asserted that there are no questions in music, and no real narrative, either, though there may be mood or sequence, we experience most significant questions as being no less sensory than music, inhabiting us even to and beyond the point of supersaturation. And yet of course, apart from at least a certain basic level of articulation achieved through cognition, there can be no questions, only vagueness (confusion, suspense, or anxiety). I envision a question as an irreducible hybrid entity that possesses some of the characteristics of sensation and thought but which is somehow more than merely the combination of the two. For Freud, however, the very presence of a certain kind of question, such as "What is the meaning of life?" was neither a sensation nor a thought, but functioned instead as a *symptom* indicating that the inquirer was ill, damaged in terms of the enjoyment of work or love.

◆

YET WHAT IS *the relationship between the question and the will, and from where in the body/brain mesh do questions arise?*

The psychiatrist Leslie H. Farber posited that every state falls into one of two realms of life—"the realm of states that can't be willed, and the realm of those that can"—and claimed that "the problem of the will lies in our recurring temptation to apply the will of the second realm to those portions of life that not only will not comply, but will become distorted under such coercion." According to Farber, "I can will knowledge, but not wisdom; going to bed, but not sleeping; eating, but not hunger; meekness, but not humility; scrupulosity, but not virtue; self-assertion or bravado, but not courage; lust, but not love; commiseration, but not sympathy; congratulations, but not admiration; religiosity, but not faith; reading, but not understanding . . . [;] speech or silence, but not conversation." I do not believe that a genuine question can be willed into being; it possesses or is possessed by something of the involuntary, as does a sensation and a thought.

In a *New York Times Magazine* article, Robin Marantz Henig explores the frontiers of brain science—in particular, current neurological work with "a particular class of brain wave known as E.R.P. or Event-Related Potential. The E.R.P. wave represents electrical activity . . . and can be a sign that high-cognitive processes . . . are taking place. . . . One thing E.R.P might eventually be able to do is predict whether someone intends to lie—even before he or she has made a decision about it." Thus, according to Jennifer Vendemia, a psychologist at the University of South Carolina who has been studying deception by looking at brain wave patterns, the test administrator would "know before you do what your brain is indicating as your intention." Is it likely that in the not-very-distant future, you will be able to view in electronic form the presence of your own questions even before they are formulated, or would the very fact of your observation skew your mental landscape in a kind of reverse time lapse? In the same article, Henig writes, "Learning to lie is an important part of maturation. What makes a child able to start telling lies, usually at about age 3 or 4, is that he has begun developing a theory of mind, the idea that what goes on in his head is different from what goes on in other people's heads." Would it be possible to lie if one were somehow physically or psychologically incapable of asking questions, and vice versa? Would it be possible to write a poem? The very presence of a lie or a question indicates that there is an "other," and that this "other" is different from the self. And the poet is one who has consciously extended, reversed, and complicated that discovery of otherness by (as I believe it was Miłosz who put it) making of his or her very self an other.

Yet even with the self as other, the questioning writer dares not remain alone inside his or her own head. The mind is drawn to the space between self and other where encounter may take place. Even our bodies know this—that's why the pulse often quickens perceptibly when one approaches one's virtual or three-dimensional mailbox. And that's what the child discovers in Randall Jarrell's poem, "A Sick Child," when his imagination addresses a question to the imagined presence of the mail carrier:

> The postman comes when I am still in bed.
> "Postman, what do you have for me today?"
> I say to him. (But really I'm in bed.)
> Then he says—what shall I have him say?
>
> "This letter says that you are president
> Of—this word here; it's a republic."
> Tell them I can't answer right away.
> "It's your duty." No, I'd rather just be sick.
>
> Then he tells me there are letters saying everything
> That I can think of that I want for them to say.
> I say, "Well, thank you very much. Good-bye."
> He is ashamed, and turns and walks away.
>
> If I can think of it, it isn't what I want.
> I want . . . I want a ship from some near star
> To land in the yard, and beings to come out
> And think to me: "So this is where you are! Come."
>
> Except that they won't do,
> I thought of them. . . . And yet somewhere there must be
> Something that's different from everything.
> All that I've never thought of—think of me!

Essayist and fiction writer Nicholson Baker once created a list of his own recurrent thoughts in order of annual frequency, some of which are questions, such as "Job, should I quit?" (34 times a year), "McCartney more talented than Lennon?" (23 times a year), and "DJ, would I be happy as one?" (9 times a year).

Like everyone else who writes, I've experienced decades of immersion in many levels and forms of poetry and in shared cultural expressions such as commercial jingles and radio hits popularly known as "ear worms" because they slip so agilely into the skull. So I'd be hard put to assign accurate frequencies to the following questions, but here, in no particular order, are a few of the ones that, perhaps for their own reasons and with their own agendas, have taken up residence in me, each waiting for the slightest of stimuli to stir it:

Why should I be my aunt, or me, or anyone? Do I contradict myself? Why should she give her bounty to the dead? What does she know of how I got trapped in my life? Who wrote the book of love? Why do fools fall in love? Why can't the English teach their children how to speak? Why so pale and wan, fond lover? Why didn't I know enough of something? Do you like green eggs and ham? What rough beast, its hour come round at last, slouches toward Bethlehem to be born? To carry the child into adult life, is it good? Oh, Mama, can this really be the end, to be stuck inside of Mobile with the Memphis blues again? What happens to a dream deferred? And hast thou slain the Jabberwock? What was that whiteness? Truth? A pebble of quartz? It's ten o'clock; do you know where your children are? Do you want to be healed? My townspeople, what are you thinking of? But when was that ever a bar to any watch they keep? Do you know the way to San Jose? Do I dare to eat a peach? Will you, won't you, will you, won't you, will you join the dance? What do women want? Who would've thought a good girl like you could destroy all my beautiful wickedness? Was he married, did he try to support, as he grew less fond of them, wife and family? Why do the nations rage? Why do stars fall down from the sky every time you walk by? Who shall say I am not the happy genius of my household? Who's the leader of the club that's made for you and me? How far is true? What is Africa to me? When we speak of God, is it God we speak of? Of those so close beside me, which are you? Which I is I? What is there to know? I'm nobody, who are you? Who is my neighbor? What, me worry? Who moved my cheese? Whom does the Grail serve? How many flies buzzed round you innocent of your grime, while you cursed the heavens of the railroad and your flower soul? Where have you been, Lord Randall, my son? What did God mean, arming him [Tony Hoagland, that is, not Lord Randall] so insufficiently, sending him into the blue part of the flame? Would I run into the fiery barn to release animals, singed and panicked, from their stalls? How many roads must a man walk down before they call him a man? O Western wind, when wilt thou blow? If I run faster, is the way shorter? Is it natural to be scattered? What is the sound of one hand clapping? What was wrong with me that I couldn't sit still the way the rest of them could? Got milk? Where's the beef? Where's Waldo? Where are the snows of yesteryear? Where have all the flowers gone? In case of emergency, does your family have a plan? How do you solve a problem like Maria? How do you spell relief? Et tu, Brute? *Voulez-vous se coucher avec moi ce soir?* What's madness but nobility of soul at odds with circumstance? Mister Postman, look and see: is there a letter in your bag for me? Who knows where the time goes? When can I go into the supermarket and buy what I need with my good looks? You think your life is over? May I call you Walt? Where are we going, Walt? [Everyone has a question for Walt!] What but design of darkness to appall? There can be a light answer to a dark question, can't there?— And one poet quotes Kramer from *Seinfeld* in her poem: "Will some of us be able to breathe underwater in the year 2000?"

I am sure that the pack of questions you've internalized via osmosis is no less varied than mine, from the most finely nuanced, painstakingly formulated rhetorical utterances to far more basic childlike inquiries that verge on belonging to the realm of demands rather than that of inquiries. Thus, I think it might be enlightening to simultaneously reverse and extend this experiment—to work toward a kind of "self-definition through negation" by compiling a list of questions that rarely or never come up for you in your life and in your writing. For instance, in my life, I have never mused, "Where would be the best place to purchase a chandelier?" or "How does one cook an artichoke?" In my poetry, I haven't engaged in very many questions to or about animals—I may be working up to that now that I live with a cat, though I doubt that I could come up with questions worthy of her. So all writers present might benefit from taking time to mentally flip through the pages of their work in search of one or two questions or kinds of questions never asked in their own poetry, either implicitly or formally—this task provides something like an anti-map of one's desires, certainly a valuable piece of equipment for any artist.

◆

WHAT HAVE WE *left behind?*

Venturing into what its owners have humbly dubbed The World Question Center [http://www.edge.org/q2010/q10_index .html] is not unlike falling into Alice's rabbit hole. A BBC radio commentator has described this website as "the crack cocaine of the thinking world." The site's announced purpose is: "[t]o arrive at the edge of the world's knowledge" by "seek[ing] out the *most* complex and sophisticated minds, put[ting] them in a room together, and hav[ing] them ask each other the questions they are asking themselves." Here you can read how intellectual luminaries like Richard Dawkins and Freeman Dyson answer such questions as "What do you believe is true even though you can't prove it?" and "What is the day's most underreported story?" Of all the questions, the one for 2001 most fascinates me, perhaps because it is a metaquestion: "What questions have disappeared?" An easy click lands you in the region of extinct or possibly extinct queries, which range from such inquiries as:

> "What happened to all that phlogiston?" "Why is
> the moon disappearing again?" "What is the best way

to prevent the soul of the deceased from reanimating this corpse?"

to

"Do I have any e-mail?" (obsolete because of the omnipresence of spam—alas, we pretty much *always* have e-mail), and "How do our brains become who we are?," which, according to NYU professor of neuroscience Joseph LeDoux, has become as good as obsolete because "[q]uestions about the neural basis of personhood, the self, have never been at the forefront of brain science, and so are not, strictly speaking, lost questions to the field." (Many would dispute this!)

Doyne Farmer, one of the founders of chaos theory, posits that all these discarded questions show us how "the evolution of knowledge is a Schumpeterian process of creative destruction, in which weeding out the questions that no longer merit attention is an integral part of formulating better questions that should. Forgetting is a vital part of creation. . . . This involves erasing information. The energy needed to do this is more than can be gained. Thus, the fact that forgetting takes work is essential to the second law of thermodynamics." And where, after all, would poetry be without entropy and loss? The psychoanalyst and literary critic Adam Phillips suggests that questions "are, among other things, the grammatical form we give to our desire" because their origin in the body is the primal delight/trauma of discovering that one is separate from one's mother, that is, the visceral experience of difference. As Dean Young says in his poem "Lives of the Painters," "if you want something, that means you're injured." In this sense, the act of questioning could never become obsolete, except perhaps in some kind of superenlightened state of consciousness, which has to do with a context different than the one I'm discussing here.

But is the highway of poetry littered with fossilized questions that contemporary poets no longer ask or bring to their work, or forms in which they no longer ask them? I can't think of any contemporary poems in which the speaker wonders without even a trace of authorial ironic distance when the fates or gods will bring his or her tribal enemies' heads on spikes. I don't see any contemporary poems wondering how to bear the absence of some version of the liege-lord, as in ancient Anglo-Saxon song. I don't see any contemporary poems in which the author nonironically seeks some authority to answer any questions in a way that would preempt or short-circuit the poet's own experience. And when I see questions that are designed to block or bypass other questions, these too tend to be presented as foils to a sense of deeper truth-seeking—"Oh, do not ask, 'What is it?' Let us go and make our visit."

This is, of course, a huge generalization, but I do think, then, that there may have been extinct questions in poetry. I see statements disguised as questions and questions disguised as statements. I see narratives as implied questions and responses, such as Albert Goldbarth's "Poem of the Praises," which I see as embodying the question: "What is the life's work of those who were never conceived?," the response being something like, "They/we push back, exert presence." I see separation/distinction seeking union/sameness, and vice versa. I see questions and objects that pose as one another, such as Stevens's jar in Tennessee, which has been interpreted and reinterpreted as many times as a piece of installation art, and its near relation, David Rivard's baby food jar filled up with the ocean in his new collection *Sugartown*.

Interestingly, I'm having troubling coming up with contemporary "ask not's." Has the face-value "ask not" become extinct? In centuries past, we have been warned to ask not for whom the bell tolls; to ask not the cause why sullen Spring so long delays her flowers to bear (in case you're wondering, it's because Chloris is gone); but in contemporary poetry, I haven't seen the upholding of any taboos regarding the act of questioning (as opposed to the field of philosophy, where the issue of what constitutes an authentic, askable question is very much alive). On the contrary, in fact, Yehuda Amichai declares, "[W]hen they told me, 'Don't ask,' / I began to ask, and I have not stopped asking since"—much in the spirit of the main character in the movie *Pi,* who says, "When I was a little kid, my mother told me not to stare into the sun. So once, when I was six, I did."

◆

PERHAPS A POETRY that celebrates the enforcement of strict cognitive boundaries is the shadow poetry of our time, by whose nonpresence all the rest of our poems are energized. However, in this poem in *Open Closed Open,* Amichai himself seems to have a complex and not entirely satisfactory relationship with the life cycle of his questions, for he goes on to say, "Oh, the small interrogatives of my life, / hopping, chirping, flitting about, / eluding me since my childhood. / Tiny as birds, light as grasshoppers. / But when I grew up, I made them into heavy affirmatives." "How can we be saved from gravity?" Amichai's dilemma seems to ask—and the response would be, "By not turning questions into 'heavy affirmatives.'" But to prod the metaphor a little, might this imply that one's questions must never grow up, one's tiny birds be somehow prevented from becoming fattened ducks, so that they'd be bonsai birds, not full-grown adults? Are those the only two possible fates for questions, or only for particular kinds of questions? Yet in a different context toward the end of the book, in the poem "Autumn, Love, Commercials," Amichai says, "From here on, bird-watchers will determine history, / geologists will plot out the future, meteorologists / will read the palm of God's hand, and botanists / will be experts in the tree of knowledge, good and evil."

This very issue of knowledge as being inextricable from death leads us to the matter of a question's embodiment in time:

Do questions come with assumptions about our experience of the nature of time?

At first glance the presence of a question within a poem's narrative might seem to imply that the narrative is driven by a linear sense of time, at least on a superficial level—first the question, and following that, the response or lack thereof. However, I find it disorienting and exhilarating to enter the world of Frank Bidart's work, where a question demands not an answer, a response, or even a sequence of further questions, but a transformation of the question itself into an action that expresses the violence, the wound at the heart of reality. Here are some of the questions posed through the central voice in "The War of Vaslav Nijinsky":

> "Should the World / *regret* the War? Should I / RE-GRET MY LIFE?"
> "DESTROY it [the world],— / or REDEEM it. // Are they the same?"

Nijinsky identifies "*the Great Questions* as "WAR and GUILT and GOD / and MADNESS . . . ," but in "The Third Hour of the Night," the sculptor Benvenuto Cellini poses a single central question, which is detonated nearly at the end of the poem: "After sex & metaphysics,— / . . . what?"

In these long poems, the response is not so much a concept as it is an action—as Bidart himself has stated that "a poem imitates an action and *is* an action." Nijinsky prays, " . . . *Let this be the Body / through which the War has passed*" and in his final performance, dances, alone, "the Nineteenth Century's / guilt, *World War One*" on January 19, 1919, so he can later announce, " . . . I HAVE EATEN THE WORLD." And Benvenuto responds to his own question ("After sex & metaphysics,— / . . . what?") with the statement "What you have made," which has *already* been enacted in the violent, fiery creation of the statue of Perseus and in the violent transformation and death of the Marunga Island woman, through which the eater becomes food and the outside becomes the inside in a never-ending cycle *"[B]ecause you have eaten and eat as eat you must / ignorant of cause or source or end."*

In these two works, question and response represent not a linear process, but a cyclical one, the act of consumption and digestion, a bloody passing back and forth between being on and of the "inside" and being on and of the "outside"—not interview or even interrogation, but predation. Anyone who dares pose a question must answer it painfully, and with nothing less than his or her own flesh. This is only one example, of course, of poetry in which embodied questioning works against linear time—there are potentially as many ways of exploring this as there are poets.

◆

GLEANINGS AND LEAVINGS (some things I think about when I think about questions):

—One of my current favorite questions is a quote from David Hockney's "On Photography": "All those attempts to bring everything in around you are part of a naïve belief that you can recreate the whole world. Well, you can't. Where would you put it? Next to the whole world?" I think about this when I use the photocopier, when I sketch, when I copy a poem or quote into my journal, when I take a photograph. Once, I broke a photocopier's plate glass in a copy shop by leaning too hard on a heavy book in order to flatten the pages. Why don't I remember what I was trying to copy, but only the sound of the glass cracking?

◆

—A BIBLICAL QUESTION: "Then Moses said, 'I will now turn aside and see this great sight, why the bush does not burn.' So when the Lord saw that he turned aside to look, God called to him from the midst of the bush and said, 'Moses, Moses!' And he said, 'Here I am.'" Does this story imply that the entire Exodus was dependent upon the presence or absence of curiosity in Moses? When we are deficient in curiosity, are we unable to hear the voice of God? What is the price of being poor in such questions, as Wittgenstein referred to being poor in categories?

◆

—MULTIPLE CHOICE: A question is—
a. a rhetorical device
b. a micro-rip in the space/time continuum
c. a vestigial tic of the dualistic mind
d. a singularity
e. a political transaction
f. a locution that precedes an answer

g.   a locution that follows an answer, as in *Jeopardy!*

h.   the serious moment when the poem begins to boil, to misquote Kenneth Koch

i.   an entity that may hide another question, also to misquote Koch

j.   other: _____

◆

—HERE IS ONE of the questions I most often ponder as I grow older: Which precious thing(s) should I leave out, since I can't do everything? Which conversations, which attempts to make life better for others, which books, which films, which walks under the sky, which attempts to organize the contents of my home, car, or office, which letters and e-mails, which desserts?

◆

—DO THE QUESTIONS of poets tend to change in any similar ways over the years? So many contemporary first books seem to deal with family and place of origin—is there any kind of common trajectory, even in the very broadest sense, from that point on?

◆

—IF IT WERE possible to divide the tribe of poets into poets of deprivation and poets of overflow—though I think it may not be, because my suspicion is that they sometimes disguise themselves as one another—how might they deploy questions differently?

◆

—WHAT ARE SOME of the differences between questions employed by poets in opposite terrestrial hemispheres? In *The Geography of Thought,* psychologist Richard Nisbett explores some of the "profound cognitive differences between Westerners and East Asians" and raises questions such as "Why do Western infants learn nouns more rapidly than verbs, when it is the other way around in East Asia?" "And if the nature of thought is not everywhere the same ... at the most basic meta-physical level," how does this fact affect "communication and rhetoric" in poetry?

◆

—ACCORDING TO NORTHWESTERN University's Dan McAdams, a pioneer in what is known as "narrative psychology," "Parents describe the past in more elaborate ways when talking to girls. When mothers talk to daughters about an unfortunate event, they are likely to provide some sort of emotional resolution, for instance, 'That was sad when your guinea pig died, but we got another one.' Boys are often left to find the emotional center themselves." How might this affect the ways in which adult males and females frame questions?

◆

—DOES MY OWN family of origin have anything to do with my fascination with questions? Does the fact that I am the daughter of two CIA agents who had multitudes of topics they could not discuss at home make me extra- or even over-curious?

◆

—WHAT MIGHT A tree of the question family look like? What might be the nature of some of the interrelationships between the question, the riddle, the koan, the enigma, the interrogation, etc.?

◆

—IN THE CONTEXT of various models of moral and/or aesthetic development, such as those of Maslow or Kohlberg, how might a hierarchy of questions be framed?

◆

—THE ULTIMATE QUESTION: Though I have always believed that that this has to do with why there is something rather than nothing, or whether or not there is a God, or what the meaning of life may be, a few years ago, I read a short science fiction story that has haunted me ever since, because it explores in a pragmatic rather than in a philosophical sense one of the most primary *components* of the ultimate question. In Greg Egan's "Reasons to Be Cheerful," a young man who has undergone severe brain damage is provided with a kind of prosthetic brain created from an international database of healthy neural structures (several thousand cadavers of individuals who had died without brain injury). For a short time, he endures a kind of universal ecstasy in which, when introduced to various stimuli during testing, it's discovered that he feels *all* of the donors' pleasures at the *highest* possible intensity—"From [all the virtual donors, he had] inherited, not the lowest common denominator, but the widest possible taste. . . . All art was sublime to [him], and all music. Every kind of food was delicious. Everyone [he] laid eyes on was a vision of perfection." Because of course this state proves just as incapacitating as his previous injury-induced state, he is then provided with a program that allows him to "control the network's refinement"— which gives him "the power to choose for [him]self, consciously and deliberately, the things that make [him] happy." With so many possibilities open to him regarding every issue—he could turn himself into any imaginable kind of personality—he falls into despair, but at the end of the story embraces the very arbitrariness that has threatened to paralyze him. As he sits with his father, he thinks:

> [H]e's there inside my head, and my mother too, and ten million ancestors, human, proto-human, remote beyond imaging. What difference did 4,000 more make? Everyone had to carve a life out of the same legacy: half universal, half particular; half sharpened by relentless natural selection, half softened by the freedom of chance. I'd just had to face the details a little more starkly.
>
> And I could go on doing it, walking the convoluted border between meaningless happiness and meaningless despair. Maybe I was lucky; maybe the

best way to cling to that narrow zone was to see clearly what lay on either side.

◆

WHY DO I think that this might be the ultimate question? Because apart from the self, however one might define "self," there is no way to even begin to engage any of the ultimate questions I mentioned earlier. You might have the lever and you might have the world, but at least in my experience, you also need some sense of identity, a place to stand—even if consists largely of knowing what you probably are not, and what you do not love. This takes us back, of course, to the questions one doesn't ask, the anti-map of desire.

Finally, I'll close by doing some violence to a passage by James Elkins from his book *The Object Stares Back*. In it, he is speaking of the art of seeing what's around us, and making a practice of observing what we might naturally tend to overlook. He repeatedly uses the word "things" in this context, but I am going to reproduce part of the passage substituting the word "questions" for the word "things":

> There are questions we do not see and questions we cannot see and questions we refuse to see, and there are also questions we can't make out, puzzling questions and sickening questions that make us wince. There are questions too boring to see, too normal or unremarkable to ever catch the eye, questions that fall through the cracks of vision, questions so odd we never figure them out, blurs, confusions, smudges, and smears. There are questions emptied of meaning because they have no use, they answer to no desire, they cannot be owned or moved or enjoyed. There are flickering questions we can't quite catch in the corner of our eye, questions that are gone when we turn our head. There are questions too brilliant to see, that sear the retina, and questions too dangerous to see, charged with frightening emotional power. There are sexual questions we might love to see but can't make ourselves look at . . . there are questions

we don't see because we don't know their names, questions we overlook every day of our lives and will continue to miss as long as we live, questions that try to get our attention and fail, and questions that hide, camouflaged and secretive questions, little questions hidden and forgotten among other questions.

♦

AND SO, I wish you a teeming universe of questions of all kinds.

STEPHEN DUNN is the author of fifteen collections
of poetry and a book of essays and memoirs
entitled *Walking Light*. In 2009, Norton published
What Goes On: Selected and New Poems 1995–2009,
his second volume of selected poems. Among
his many awards are the Pulitzer Prize and the
Paterson Prize for Sustained Literary Achievement.
He lives in Frostburg, Maryland, with his wife, the
writer Barbara Hurd.

Dunn was a featured writer at the 2002 Ohio
University Spring Literary Festival.

The Poem, Its Buried Subject, and the Revisionist Reader

Behind "The Guardian Angel"

STEPHEN DUNN

TO REVISIT AN OLD POEM OF yours is often to come to it as an interested stranger. By degree, you're more reader than author, and like all readers you bring to the poem an aesthetic and a psychology forged by personal history and your history of reading. If twenty years have elapsed since you've written a poem about a certain kind of spiritual endurance, and in the meantime you've become, say, a communist and have turned almost exclusively to reading poems for their political significance, then you're likely that poem's revisionist. Even if you've remained roughly the same, the world around you hasn't, and inevitably provides you with a slightly different angle of regard. The good reader works hard at trying to compensate for these vicissitudes, tries to give each poem a fair trial and a fair sentence, though the writer as reader of his own poem may still be clinging—perhaps even rightly so—to some old allegiances. But one thing is sure: As author, no matter how well you've blended your intentions with your discoveries, the reader always completes your poem.

At first, I found this intolerable, like someone renaming my child. And, I confess, it remains intolerable much of the time. But. So much that's instructive begins with *but*.

Moreover, if I agree with Stendhal, and I do, "that speech was given to man to conceal his thoughts," then I shouldn't have been very much surprised that my poem "The Guardian Angel," or any poem, for that matter, might have an elusive subtext. But I was surprised.

No, I hadn't become a communist, but twenty years did elapse before I revisited "The Guardian Angel," enough time for me to witness the poem differently. Almost instantly, there it was—the buried subject—hiding like much of the world itself, not far from the surface.

More often than not, to be wholly unaware of what's driving your poem means that you're listening to the wrong cues, and therefore likely to make poor choices. You think you're writing about *that time she left me,* but fail to realize that your poem might simultaneously need to be exploring the nature of loss. You're following the lesser drift. You need to revise, but as long as the deeper subject remains hidden you're only thinking cosmetically, just shifting a few words around. Or, what you allow yourself to think of as subtlety is really just a kind of avoidance, an unconscious refusal to enter certain delicate territory. Or, even more typically these days, you're in the headlong process of composing associatively, disparate image following disparate image, but never seem to arrive at the poem's locus of concern. You're dazzling, you're on your way to postmodernist heaven, but you've yet to find a principle of selection; almost anything can be substituted for anything else. The radical entry into your subject eludes you. Your poem has taken its place among the many casualties of indulgence and unconsciousness.

But here's the paradox. Successful poems are often written with a similar unconsciousness. Buried subjects, for example, even when they are the products of inattention or avoidance, can give poems a behind-the-scenes radiance. "The Guardian Angel," I'm quite sure, is one of those poems that profited by what I didn't know about it. What follows—this retrospective foray into the making of a poem—will be a re-creation, thus a fiction, which is to say it's interested in approximating the truth. With luck, it'll live as the poem's good companion, casting some light and maybe a few shadows.

Trust the tale, not the teller, D. H. Lawrence admonishes. I'm aware of such wisdom. *But.* But, on the other hand, let me say that I wish for you to trust everything I say. This is just to let you know I'm not without guile or strategy.

Here, finally, is the poem:

The Guardian Angel

Afloat between lives and stale truths,
   he realizes
he's never truly protected one soul,

they all die anyway, and what good
   is solace,
solace is cheap. The signs are clear:

the drooping wings, the shameless thinking
   about utility
and self. It's time to stop.

The guardian angel lives for a month
   with other angels,
sings the angelic songs, is reminded

that he doesn't have a human choice.
   The angel of love
lies down with him, and loving

restores to him his pure heart.
   Yet how hard it is
to descend into sadness once more.

When the poor are evicted, he stands
   between them
and the bank, but the bank sees nothing

in its way. When the meek are overpowered
  he's there, the thin air
through which they fall. Without effect

he keeps getting in the way of insults.
  He keeps wrapping
his wings around those in the cold.

Even his lamentations are unheard,
  though now,
in for the long haul, trying to live

beyond despair, he believes, he needs
  to believe
everything he does takes root, hums

beneath the surfaces of the world.

I like to talk about the composition of poems as involv-
ing a series of allegiances that we keep as long as we can,
but which we modify and refine as the language we employ
starts to make its own demands. In "The Guardian Angel,"
my initial allegiance was to creating a secular angel, an allegiance I gradually abandoned. Instead, I found myself with
a disaffected guardian angel, the poem's first real discovery. I
vaguely remember discarding all the language and claims (two
or three stanzas worth of warm-up) that had gotten me to that
discovery, and beginning right away with his disaffectedness.
"Afloat between lives and stale truths, / he realizes / he's never
truly protected one soul." I was in a "what if" poem. What if
there were such a thing as a disaffected angel? How would he
act? What would he be thinking? I had two allegiances now,
to the serious playfulness of executing his disaffection, and to
finding an imaginative logic for it. A drama was unfolding. He
was, by definition, a do-gooder, who now was thinking only
of self. Worse, he was thinking of results, as if he could be the
arbiter of what a result was. Wasn't that for Someone else to
decide? I was starting to become interested in him. But only in

him. I had no idea that something else might also be driving the poem.

I suppose the next lines became available to me because I was at a writers' colony. The angel seeks out his own kind, is restored by them, especially by the angel of love who, by example, is able to remind him of generosity and its worth. Prior to these moments, my compositional possibilities were wide open. Now I had narrowed them by choosing to have him healed. He might have been an interesting renegade, confrontational and subversive, disruptive of the established order. He might have wanted a new identity, an angel's job that required less of him. I'm sure I could have written in either of those directions as well as in others. We learn, as Roethke says, by going where we go.

I can't remember if, around this time, I knew that I was taking him on a rather classical religious journey—that he would lose his way before he found his way, that some kind of passage was being enacted. Certainly it was apparent to me later. What I did know at the time was that play had gotten me beyond the purely fanciful; that is, beyond the pleasures of invention, beyond, say, the poem as exercise. I had arrived at some principle of selection, something that could help me find the poem's next moments: the guardian angel would not quit, it wasn't one of his choices. Nevertheless, I recognized how difficult it would be for him "to descend into sadness once more." I only half-knew where I was going, and therefore could still avoid the perils of purposefulness, could ride some uncodified energy. In retrospect, these were my new allegiances: to the poem's adjusted original impulse; to the texture, sounds, and rhythms of the language used so far; and to the unknowns of this new, governing drift.

I wasn't conscious of needing to come up with a series of tests for his newfound resolve, but that's what I found myself doing. Okay, he returns to earth and to his job. What's likely to be his experience? Certainly, if the poem were to stay in the realm of the probable, he would once again fail. But I was as much committed to the poem's rhythmical recurrences as I was to the recurrences of his ineffectuality, and may have known there couldn't be the latter without the former. I had begun to feel for him, and the rhythm had to authenticate this. Which is to say that content decisions were inseparable from decisions about syntax and flow, and were just a part of the overall orchestration of effects. Earlier, perhaps, I could have let content drive the poem. But no longer. Of course there were still various content options available to me. I could have allowed him, for example, one success. That would have set the poem on a slightly different course. In this case, what I ended up *not* selecting proved instructive. It, too, pointed the way.

The poem was leaning into its structure, though hadn't yet found its true form, if form, as Levertov says, is the revelation of content. (At the time I frequently used that step-down, three-line stanza to harness and discipline my discursive inclinations. Initially, it was an editing device, to help identify and abolish excess content. It would evolve into a way of thinking about the poem as architecture. That is, as something that would seek its shape, stanza by stanza, by an acute attention to its inner relationships.) Structurally, thus far, the poem had three movements: the introduction of the disaffected angel, his resurrection into new resolve, and his return to duty, which proved no more successful than before. Whatever mixture of intellection and obsession was driving the poem was now calling for a fourth movement, and thus would take me toward the often illusory world of closure. The poet's temperament and compositional tics are always involved in that mysterious world, but since they're usually the last things we can do anything about, it's better instead to be as alert as possible to the poem's overt promptings. I tried to be. But by this time my choices, to a significant degree, were being made for me. I was both creator and responder to my creation. I'm not sure if I ever consciously *chose* to have the guardian angel live with his ineffectualness.

Nor did I ever consider having him quit again, which now seems a reasonable option. It just felt right, I suppose, to have him persevere in spite of repeated failure. At the moment, I knew I had moved him from disaffection, but to what? Acceptance? Resignation? A desperate hopefulness? Some instructive thread would need to be pulled through if closure were to take the poem to what could feel like its inevitability.

Well, that's one fiction, one way to speculate about what I found myself doing. Another, which will be even less coherent and therefore, I think, closer to the truth, is that the poem was composed during many sittings, had many false starts, much extraneous language, and stanzas in various orders. Parts of it, I vaguely recall, were cargoed in from other poems, those failed poems most of us save and steal from. I revised it over a period of months, and many of the revisions were arrived at, as I said before, because of the exigencies of rhythm and the seeking of cooperative sounds, determining what weight of language a stanza could bear, and other considerations that had more to do with problem solving than with genesis or willfulness. At some point, that hint of a thread, that elusive something, famously invisible when the poem isn't on the right course, appeared. The angel, "in for the long haul," could not *not* be who he was. As it turns out, it was only a semblance of the real thread, but finding the ghost of it enabled me, I think, to create an illusion of orderliness and authority. Such a thread starts to become visible the more a poem's surface felicities get in some concordance with the pulse of its undercurrents.

Now, having said this, I recognize that from the start I was the god of this universe made of words, and had considerable time before book publication—cool, considered time—to assay and evaluate all of my choices, conscious and unconscious. I am responsible for everything in it, and could have, had I been fool-ishly or even perhaps wisely willful, changed its direction, pulled the thread through to a different conclusion, made the poem happier, sadder, etc. But my overriding allegiance was to the poem as a whole, to my fiction and its interlocking parts, and to how they held up for examination their revelations and con-cealments. Finally, we leave or abandon our poems because no more aesthetic decisions seem available to us that will help enact or explore our subject. At least I could think of none before "The Guardian Angel" found its way into my book *Between Angels*.

But "finally" is premature. Twenty years after the poem was written, I was visiting a colleague's class in which some of my poems were under discussion. She was, in fact, teaching *Between Angels,* and one of her students asked if I could read and comment on "The Guardian Angel." I hadn't read the poem in a while, and as I read it, it seemed clear to me what my buried subject had been, though I hadn't known it had a buried subject. Was I seeing what was truly there, or was I bringing new urgencies to an old poem that somehow permitted them to be entertained? It's true that at the time of the rereading I had been preoccupied with the generation of poets in love with the romance of self-destruction, the generation of Berryman and Schwartz and Jarrell, to name just a few, and how so few of them made it out of their fifties. And it's true that I had begun to wonder about myself in that regard. I remember smiling as I told the class that the poem is an analogue of the poet's condition in America. The poet does his job, I said, and hardly anybody listens or cares. All his life he lives with his ineffectuality, his invisible presence, the reality that there's little evidence that he makes anything happen. But

> . . . trying to live
>
> beyond despair, he believes, he needs
>   to believe
> everything he does takes root, hums
>
> beneath the surfaces of the world.

There it was, my dogged optimism, my little anthem for continuing on. This "what if" poem, this verbal construct that had found out just enough about itself to sustain the angel's journey from disaffection to endurance, was a personal poem after all. The buried subject, I was sure now, had been the poem's co-driving force, and its secret glue.

But wait. Even if what I just said is persuasive, there's one more wrinkle. If the poem's hidden subject and the thread I pulled through are similar, as they now seem to have been, how can I have pulled through a thread I didn't become conscious of until years later? One answer, as I've suggested, is that the making of a poem is a constant compromise between the author's intent and the discoveries that confound it, that this process itself is a kind of decision maker, has its own intelligence, and is more alert to undercurrents than I could have been. Another is that there's no answer, just more or less plausible fictions, and this entire essay constitutes one of them. Or that, in fact, I did it, I pulled the secret thread down and through while thinking only of an angel's problems and how to arrange them, and that such things happen all the time, and take their not unfamiliar places among the mysteries of composition.

Trust the tale.

LEE K. ABBOTT is the author of seven collections of short stories, most recently *All Things, All at Once: New & Selected Stories.* His fiction has appeared in nearly one hundred periodicals, including *Harper's,* the *Atlantic,* the *Georgia Review, Epoch,* the *Southern Review,* and *Boulevard.* His work has been reprinted in *The Best American Short Stories, The O. Henry Awards: The Prize Stories,* The Best of the West series, and the Pushcart Prize series. Twice a winner of fellowships from the National Endowment for the Arts, he has published essays and reviews in the *New York Times Book Review,* the *Miami Herald,* the *Chicago Tribune,* and the *Los Angeles Times Book Review.* He is Arts & Humanities Distinguished Professor in English at the Ohio State University, where he directs the MFA Program in Creative Writing.

Abbott was a featured writer at the 2008 Ohio University Spring Literary Festival.

Thirteen Things about the Contemporary Short Story That Really Hack Me Off

LEE K. ABBOTT

IN THE EARLY '80S, I STUMBLED upon *The Secret Life of Our Times,* a volume of short stories edited by the infamous Gordon Lish when he was the literary editor at *Esquire,* indisputably one of the most influential periodicals of that and any period. It included stories by such heavyweights as Márquez, Carver, DeLillo, and so on—a who's who, if you will, of those in the day going short. It also included—best of all, from my point of view—an introduction, "The Poetics of Fiction," by Tom Wolfe. (A digression, of which there will be more than a few henceforth: I'm working from memory here, the book in question having disappeared from my shelves; I have the habit, not bad at all, of loaning books to students, this one included; evidently, it's not been returned, and owing to being the cheapskate I am and still hopeful that the book will find its way back to me, I refuse to pay a zillion dollars to those still in possession of what's described as a "rare" book.) Reading between the lines separating those of Mr. Lish and those of Mr. Wolfe, one can only conclude that the latter hated the former's taste, for Mr. Wolfe's "reading" of these stories results in an essay noteworthy for its disappointment and its ire.

Mr. Wolfe argues that, during this era in American letters, we'd reached the, er, poetic period, a time when much that had been true about fiction, the short story in particular, seemed no longer applicable. Specifically, he articulated features of the contemporary story that flew in the face of convention and tradition. Stories, for example, were no longer unbroken narratives from "Once upon a time" to "The End." Rather, they were broken—"fractured," to be less forgiving—into blocks of type separated by white space, what he calls, as something akin to the stanza (or strophe, for you fussy sorts), "crots" (a wonderful term I urge you to use often in mixed company). In addition, stories seemed to happen nowhere—on an island, in a forest, near a lake—places abstract and vague and, one supposes, putatively "universal" (a word I urge no one to use with a straight face). His big discovery was that characters suffered from "unnamed dread" (which is as sad as it is laughable: not the discovery, mind you, but the discovered; me, I know what afflicts, as, I bet do you: It's the girl who won't love you, it's the parent dying slowly and painfully, it's the fear in a combat zone, it's—well, to the ordinary among us who have to live life rather than write about it, "dread" has a face, a name, a zip code, a PDA, and a desire to play drums in a band called Dr. Filth and the Leather Cup). In any event, at the end of his essay, Mr. Wolfe dismissed the stories in question as shallow, silly, goofy, and happily forgettable—Proust, Cortázar, Joyce, and Beckett knockoffs (though I still have a lot of affection for DeLillo's "In the Men's Room of the Sixteenth Century," a postapocalyptic hoot: Mad Max meets Walt Whitman and the Ayatollah of Rock'n'Rolla). Literature Lite, amigos. Typing, not tale telling. The end, methought, seemed nigh.

And today, alas, it's nigher still. (Bear with me, please. I'll get to the name-calling and finger-pointing soon.) Every fourth year for the last twelve, I've taught a graduate seminar that I call

"Form and Theory of the Short Story," and every time I teach it I teach it with the same question in mind: is there an aesthetic in the contemporary short story? That is, is there something, or are there some things, that most writers nowadays do between margins? (Crots, for instance, are, like the poor, still with us.) For my texts, I use the most recent three editions of the *Best American Short Stories* or *The Prize Stories: The O. Henry Awards.* (I know, I know: not scientific, you say; not representative; not a large enough sampling; not inclusive enough. To which complaints, I shrug and say, "Get your own darn class to teach.") Each year we read, oh, forty to fifty stories. And each year, we make a list of those habits of mind that at least a majority of the writers collected in those esteemed volumes seem to have in common. Trends, not tics. Manners and methods. Sensibilities, if not sense. Proclivities. Vocabulary, not idiom. And each year, lo and behold, we make discoveries similar to Mr. Wolfe's own, and, like him (I'm the Russian judge, of course), we are aggravated, annoyed, flummoxed, and saddened by our conclusions. Herewith, then, the results (in no particular order).

◆

1. CHARACTERS DON'T work. Wait, let me rephrase that. Characters may have jobs, but we never see them doing them (notable exception: teachers; we see lots of stories about teachers, probably because many of us "willing the word" are teachers). Roughly speaking, only 6 or 7 percent of the workforce is unemployed in America, yet few stories take place at work. Few stories in factories. Few stories at the supermarket. No stories in banks (unless, of course, you've gone there to rob one). TV and movies have exploited the workplace for drama for years. *Mad Men. Law & Order. House.* We have, I think, forsaken the public place for the more private: the bedroom, the kitchen, the backyard. (Another digression: I exaggerate, to be sure, and I do so both to get your attention and to make my point, so if you're thinking of the five hundred stories that happen at the Swift Packaging Plant in Omaha, keep your mutterings to yourself. I didn't promise you science; I promised you preaching. The sky is falling, ladies and germs, and I am not going to stand here arguing parts per million.)

◆

2. IN 1970, I spent one miserable semester in the MFA Program at Columbia University (the particulars of which I shall amuse you with another time). Among my teachers were two distinguished African American writers, John A. Williams and John Oliver Killens. And, Lordy, were they steamed. A season or two before, William Styron had published *The Confessions of Nat Turner,* a novel in which the narrator is Nat Turner himself in the first-person point of view. Mr. Williams and Mr. Killens, along with nine other black writers, responded with *Eleven Black Writers Respond,* a volume of essays that seemed to argue but one point: How dare Styron, a white writer, steal our material. It was an argument then that puzzled; it continues to puzzle. I prefer the notion offered by Henry James: "execution" is the measure of excellence. Such has nothing to do with gender, ethnicity, religion, creed, able-bodiedness, sexual orientation, or any other category that means to silence or marginalize writers. Moreover, I think it's in the best interests of the republic—yes, the body politic—for us, courtesy of the page, to inhabit what the pointy-headed of another critical era called The Other. Still, I find, among the scribblers we read for the seminar, little writing "out of kind." Black writers have black protagonists, women women, gay gay—which, to my mind, is solipsism of a most unproductive, even dangerous, sort.

◆

3. MENNONITES! WHICH in one class became "code" for the nearly rampant use of the *deus ex machina,* a creaky literary device that, if it says anything at all, says, "Help, I've fallen and I can't get up." Here's the specific: story begins with hero in a pickle; plot thickens nicely, more pickly; and then, at the point where the pickle is the pickliest, what to our wondering eyes appear, most conveniently, but a group of handy and helpful Mennonites whose presence leads directly to the tidiest of resolutions. Such, I hold, is sin—mortal sin (to continue with the submerged metaphor). If the writer needed the Mennonites to arrive in order to fix the story, then, Jumpin' Jesus, we readers should've known they existed within the world of the story

(headline in *Daily Planet* in first page of story: "Mennonites Land! Headed Your Way"). If, by contrast, the writer wanted to employ "god's machine," then its appearance should have been made inevitable rather than merely fortuitous (see Ron Carlson's "Phenomenon" for its artfulness with this approach).

◆

4. WRITERS RESCUE characters from themselves. I've done this, I confess. In a story called "One of *Star Wars,* One of *Doom,*" my attempt to understand school shootings (think Columbine), I needed to get one of my major characters, a male history teacher, to the math wing of the high school so that he might be shot. He's married, but has a lover, a younger woman algebra teacher. For the longest time—several drafts, in fact; I am, clearly, a slow learner—his motivation for venturing toward the numbers was that he would apologize to his girlfriend for, among other crimes against decency, taking her for granted. Then I had the lucky insight that, no, this guy doesn't apologize. He's a jerk. He's hoping to get some tail during free period, at the very least some heavy petting. Simply put, I had wanted him to be better than he was. I had, because I root mightily for the best in our crooked kind, wanted to save him from himself. Writers, I argue, are good people. Isn't one of the reasons we visit the page again and again because of our love of the tribe? Not surprisingly, then, we redeem the unredeemable, even at the expense of the credible or the possible.

◆

5. FEW FUNNY stories. Read *Without Feathers* by Woody Allen and ask yourself if, in another's pages you're reading, you spend any time at all laughing the way you do when you read "A Brief History of Organized Crime." I bet not. Instead, we are encouraged to be, gulp, serious. Serious writers are taken—you saw this coming, right?—more seriously. They're *artistes,* not knuckleheaded goofballs. Yet all around us—on TV, in the movies, on stage—we find and applaud the comic. I don't understand. Shoot, I'd settle for the wry, the rueful, the amused, the lighthearted, the risible. Some days, I'd settle for merely the spirited over what, in brief, we see too much of nowadays: the dour, the achingly earnest, the MEANINGFUL.

♦

6. ALMOST NO use of the omniscient third person point of view. Richard Russo, he of *Nobody's Fool* and *Paradise Falls,* among other books, has argued that the third person omniscient is probably the point of view we should be telling most of our stories from. I don't know about that, but I do think that I can count on the fingers of one hand the third omniscient stories I've read in the last ten years. Artistically, Mr. Russo does have a point: God's view of our hurly-burly is the wisest and the most liberating. For the school-shooting story I referenced above, I tried it, albeit unwittingly. I had no plans to report on high about the "imagined real world." Then, lo and verily, there it was, the first line: *The slaughter hasn't happened yet.* What I discovered thereafter was that as a writer I got, at last, the chance to use the two oldest moves in the trade (they may even be the same move—you decide): *meanwhile, back at the ranch* and *little did he know.*

♦

7. TOO MUCH present tense. For a certain generation of writer—all right: the fuddy-duddy, me among them—telling a story in the present tense is too trendy by half. It results, so would opine the mossback, in "foregrounding," the sense that you as a reader are being constantly reminded that you're reading writing. In other words, you are not being invited into the illusion; you're being distanced from it. You're not being educed to experience the drama; you're being obliged to observe it. The best argument against its use is presented by William Gass in his essay "A Failing Grade for the Present Tense." (The present tense, he writes, "is like walking through a cemetery before they've put in the graves.") My view is that too many writers use the present tense to demonstrate how hip they are. Their contention is that the present tense is, well, more urgent, more immediate. To which contention I say, as politely as possible, "nonsense." It's annoying, precious, self-consciously arty-farty (yet, even as I rant, I will remind all that John Updike, more fuddy than not, wrote all the Rabbit books in the present tense).

♦

8. THE SECOND person point of view is rarely used. Its artificiality is obvious, a liability except in the hands of writers

who use it as "marker" for the first person (e.g., Lori Moore, Junot Diaz, Jay McInerney). *You are walking down the street,* the writer has typed. To which I answer, "No, I'm not. I'm sitting at my desk, story in hand." Still, I will admit to having tried my hand, though I did complicate the issue for myself by doing so in the subjunctive mood (the story is called—get this—"As Fate Would Have It"). Is there a contradiction here? Yup: I am nothing if not one with both Donnie and Marie (a little bit country *and* a little bit rock'n'roll). Indeed, I side with Walt Whitman on the matter: "Do I contradict myself? Well, then, I contradict myself."

◆

9. THE PAGE 2 move. You've seen this strategy a zillion times, I bet. Writer establishes the dramatic present—what's going on and who to root for (though not necessarily why you should root in the first place, which is what Henry James calls "the stout stake of emotion"). Then, without so much as a "by your leave," writer suspends the forward momentum of story to give us—often on the second page, sometimes in the second paragraph—backstory. Sometimes this backstory comes in the form of flashback; less felicitously, it comes to us as exposition—lots and lots and lots of exposition—before the writer returns to the dramatic present. This, folks, is plain aggravating. The genius of story is brevity. Stories, in addition, succeed by what they leave out. One detail must do the work of ten. I must only know what plays a motive role in the outcome of the yarn. Get on with it, already!

◆

10. WHERE ARE our stylists? On the continuum of style, from Hemingway to Faulkner (from min- to max-, in other words), we have more Carvers than Nabokovs. I wonder if contemporary writers have lost their appetites for the riches peculiar to our medium, language. Whither the complex-compound sentence? The elliptical sentence, parallel structure, subordination, coordination—animals rarely sighted. The way of the dodo has gone the periodic sentence. I miss anaphora, chiasmus, diacope, metanoia. I yearn for zeugma, hyperbaton, aporia. Come back, epistrophe. Please. (A subset of this complaint is my notion that

the metaphor is disappearing, fewer and fewer writers keen to hitch, as I. A. Richards put it, tenor to vehicle.)

◆

11. IF SOME writers give us too much past (and at just the wrong time: see gripe #9), some give us too little (or, gulp, none). That's right: no parents, no pets, no partners. We get feelings, actions, and thoughts (aka: the FAT theory of fiction that I am so tickled with), but few facts. Characters seem not to have had a life before the writer typed out her version of "Once upon a time." Too many protagonists are without a banker, bills to pay, or a vacation in the third grade to Disneyland. Where is the irksome neighbor with the mullet? Who is the plumber of record? What happened to those five years in a Turkish prison? Is there a sock drawer we need to hear about? My point is that a character does not arrive in the dramatic present without deep and permanent attachments to everything that has theretofore befallen him.

◆

12. MUTED CLIMAX. As an undergraduate, I was "raised" by the pulp writer James Mealy (not a name I expect anyone except a few Aggies to recognize). Jim wrote for *True Confession* and its ilk. Stories like "Martians Made Me Their Love Slave." In short, he didn't care about my ideas, my impossibly juvenile notions of Serious Li-Tra-Chure. Rather, he was concerned with my growth as a craftsman, a writer who could expeditiously get from the garage to the kitchen without accounting for every nick in the paint. His was a concern for the nuts and bolts—when to tell, for example, when to show. Of special concern to him was the climax, our most dramatic moment. Nowadays, stories don't seem to end with a bang; instead, they seem to dribble to a close. Climax has been shortened, subdued. He suggested that climax should be four double-spaced pages at a minimum. Because, scenically, climax has the most at stake, it should be the most thoroughly rendered. I like Perry Smith's observation: "Let's put some hair on the walls." Yeah, let's.

◆

13. EPIPHANY, SIGH, is still with us. Phil Lopate has a wonderful essay, "Always Be Closing," that argues that the contemporary story writer is too much in thrall to three saints: Saint Anton (Chekhov), Saint James (Joyce), and Saint Raymond (Carver). On the tyranny of the epiphany, courtesy of Joyce, I agree. Too much insight, I say, most of it unearned, most of it phony (and obvious) as a clown's red nose. I am reminded of this joke: A fellow hears that there is a mystic in the mountains of Tibet so undertakes a journey to get his counsel, which puts him in harm's way at nearly every turn—terrible weather, forbidding terrain, hostile natives; finally, after months of trial and deprivation, fellow hauls himself up the correct mountain, confronts said wise man. "Tell me," he says, "what is the meaning of life?" The mystic, bearded and berobed, fixes the fellow with a stare straight from science fiction. "Life," he intones, "is a well." Our hero is stunned. He pulls his hair, gnashes what needs gnashing. He recounts his journey, the many perils, the many horrors he suffered. "And you're telling me," he concludes, "that life is a well?" To which the mystic answers, "You mean it's not?" Precisely. That epiphany you're having? It's gas. It, too, shall pass.

◆

OKAY, ENOUGH. I will say that I fret over plot, in particular its disassociation from character. I worry, too, about an inattention to form (another way of making meaning, according to Mark Schorer). Place, methinks, has never been more crucial, for it is, as Miss Welty reminds us, "the crossroads of time and character." I fret about beginnings, specifically those that have me, at the end of the first page, muttering, "So what?" I wring my hands, I pace, I gaze too often into my own navel. Let, in short, the conversation begin. I want to hear from you.

TONY HOAGLAND is the author of numerous books of poetry, including *Unincorporated Persons in the Late Honda Dynasty* and *What Narcissism Means to Me,* a finalist for the National Book Critics Award in poetry in 2004. He has received many awards for writing, including the Jackson Poetry Prize, the O. B. Hardisson Award, and the Mark Twain Award. In 2005 his book of essays about poetry and craft, *Real Sofistakashun,* was published by Graywolf. He teaches in the writing program at the University of Houston and in the Warren Wilson low-residency MFA program.

Hoagland was a featured writer at the 2008 Ohio University Spring Literary Festival.

Litany, Gamesmanship, and Representation

Charting the Old to the New Poetry

T O N Y H O A G L A N D

The old poetry can be about willows;
Haiku requires crows picking snails
    in a rice paddy.

> —Basho, announcing the new aesthetics,
> circa AD 700

Epistemology and theories of language—how
we know what we know, how we say it—have
become as central to contemporary lyric
as psychoanalysis in the late 50s, myth and
politics in the late 60s.

> —Stephen Burt, "The Elliptical Poets,"
> *American Letters and Commentary*

A S A M E R I C A N P O E T S A N D
poetry readers, we find ourselves in the midst of the third wave
of poetic modernism, when American poetry is exploding into
a galaxy of formal experiment and innovation. All manner of
things drift under the poetic sun, from diction-saturated abcdar-
ium poems to fragmentary metaphysical minimalism. Because
we are in its midst, we aren't sure yet of its nature, its meanings,
its idioms, or how to assign value to its productions. Is it camp?

Is it absurdist? Is it defiantly detached, self-preoccupiedly mannerist clever coterie poetry? Is it self-defeatingly sophisticated? Is it the inauguration of an amazing new physics of representation? We just can't tell yet.

One place to begin is to consider the evolution, in the last sixty years, of the poet's relationship to the word. This essay will review and explore the course of those changes by considering a series of examples of the litany. Because the litany, by definition, is a poetic form dedicated to the act of naming, it provides a useful source for sampling the changing perspective of the poet upon language itself.

In his ninth *Duino Elegy,* Rilke hypothesizes that the cosmic purpose of human beings on earth, surprisingly enough, might not be procreation, but speech:

> Are we, perhaps, here just for saying: *House,*
> *Bridge, Fountain, Jug, Olive Tree, Window,*—
> possibly: *Pillar, Tower?* . . . but for saying, remember,
> oh for such saying as never the things themselves
> hoped so intensely to be.

Rilke suggests a vocation for poets: a kind of stewardship. The poet names, and her/his speech vivifies reality (*olive tree, window*) by pronouncing it. To name is to recognize and endorse material reality, to *encourage* it, and at the same time to illuminate and spiritualize it. The Biblical resonance—to Adam's act of assigning the first names—is evident, and like *that* story, Rilke's scenario suggests a sacred relationship, which places into transaction three elements: the poet, the word, and the thing. Man is redeemed by the unique usefulness of his speech; matter is elevated by recognition; speech holds unique value for its precision and responsiveness. Here, there is no hint of misfit between words and things—no inaccuracy, and no misrepresentation. Rilke implies that the cosmic breach between spirit and matter can be healed when we embrace, through our speech, the whole world of creation.

This confidence about the functional harmony between speech, things, and humans has not remained constant. In the twentieth century, our faith in the adequacy of language has shifted nervously around again and again, as has our belief in the reliability of knowledge, perception, and human nature. If we want to see how poetry has changed in the last sixty years, we can learn a lot by looking at how the poet's relationship to the word has continued to change. The literary form of the litany, because it engages in a kind of ceremonial naming, like the one proposed by Rilke's poem, offers an ideal poetical prototype from which to draw examples of how naming changes.

Rilke's poem proposes an almost premodern model for poetry's relationship to the word: perception, recognition, endorsement. We poet-humans are allowed to frolic in the naming of the world. Something like what the British poet Christopher Smart might have been feeling when he sang a pre-Whitman ode to his housecat.

> For I will consider my Cat Jeoffry.
> For he is the servant of the Living God, duly and daily
>   serving him.
> For at the first glance of the glory of God in the East he
>   worships in his way.
> For is this done by wreathing his body seven times
>   round with elegant quickness.
> For then he leaps up to catch the musk, which is the
>   blessing of God upon his prayer.
> For he rolls upon prank to work it in.
> For having done duty and received blessing he begins to
>   consider himself.
> For this he performs in ten degrees.
> For first he looks upon his forepaws to see if they are clean.
> For secondly he kicks up behind to clear away there.
> For thirdly he works it upon stretch with the forepaws
>   extended.
> For fourthly he sharpens his paws by wood.
> For fifthly he washes himself.
> For sixthly he rolls upon wash.
> For seventhly he fleas himself, that he may not be
>   interrupted upon the beat.
> For eighthly he rubs himself against a post.

(Jubilate Agno, Fragment B, lines 695–710)

Smart's litany illustrates a set of premises about poetic speech: in the meticulousness of his observation, he reveals a faith in the ability of language to precisely convey; likewise, he believes in the obligation of the psalmist to be accurate in his depictions. Thirdly, the poet of *Jubilate Agno* is allowed some inventiveness—licensed to add verbal and imaginative flourishes, which, in this context, act to mimic the gusto of the cat itself, as well as enact the delight of the speaker. As postmodern, more self-conscious writers, we can admire Smart's lack of inhibition, his confidence that words are enough; that the world does not revolt against being named; nor do words betray material reality. The result is an athletic song of praise with both naturalness and literary flourish.

But scroll forward through the anthology of years, and consider the contemporary poem "Wildflower," by Stanley Plumly. Like the previous examples, "Wildflower" is a poem of loving praise, and a poem in contact with the sensory universe of nature. But it is also a poem into which linguistic insecurity has entered: a poem which has been forced to make the flawed, slippery act of naming part of its subject matter, part of its approach to "truth":

> It is June, wildflowers on the table.
> They are fresh an hour ago, like sliced lemons,
> with the whole day ahead of them.
> They could be common mayflower lilies of the valley,
>
> day lilies, or the clustering Canada, large, gold,
> long-stemmed as pasture roses, belled out over the vase—
> or maybe Solomon's seal, the petals
> ranged in small toy pairs
>
> or starry, tipped at the head like weeds.
> They could be anonymous as weeds.
> They are, in fact, the several names of the same thing,
> lilies of the field, butter-and-eggs,
>
> toadflax almost, the way the whites and yellows juxtapose,
> and have "the look of flowers that are looked at,"
> rooted as they are in water, glass, and air.
> I remember the summer I picked everything,
>
> flower and wildflower, singled them out in jars
> with a name attached.

Plumly's litany of naming is a ritual of praise, but not just praise: it also turns on the topic of lost youth, which is synonymous with lost certainty. There was a day in which the speaker knew the names of things, and trusted them—when everything had "a name attached." But now a gulf has opened between himself and things. The older, less trusting, and less trustworthy, speaker names the flowers as if stabbing at something he can't get exactly right. Thus the poem tells the tale of a double fall from grace—not just from youth into the uncertainty of adulthood, into alienation, but also into the situation of knowing oneself to be disconnected from the creation. The estrangement from self and the estrangement from language have become symptomatic of each other. It seems appropriate that the speaker, mid-poem, cites T. S. Eliot's wry, cross-eyed description of flowers: "the flowers have the look of flowers that are looked at." A gulf has opened between words and things. In this postnatural existence, once man is lost in the maze of self-consciousness, all things recede into the distant mirror. It is impossible to get any closer to X than the sign for X.

Plumly's speaker-poet has a case of language cross-eyes, a modern bifocal condition that has only worsened for poets over the last thirty years, this double vision that can lead to a host of speech impediments like stuttering, dyslexia, and muteness. The next generation of poets would contract a case of dislocation influenza that makes Plumly's linguistic uneasiness look like the sniffles.

Some Background Perspective

This might be a useful moment in which to introduce a few background contexts. Plumly's speaker, ill at ease in the world, deficient both linguistically (in naming) and epistemologically (in knowing), is emblematic of a culturewide modern condition. We have never mistrusted language more than in our postmodern era. Not only that, we have never so mistrusted the art of "knowing" itself. As the first line of a John Ashbery poem declares, "You can't say it that way any more." The gap between words and things, and between words and "truth," has never been more conspicuous. Our trust in the reliability of representation has never been more fragile and paradoxical. We have a general sense of instability, of indeterminacy; and we feel the impermanence and probable imperfection of any kind of knowing.

In addition to whatever existential causes there might be for this condition, media and consumer culture have contributed heavily to erode and corrupt our faith in language. Most of the language we encounter in daily life deploys some manipulation, and conceals some motive. Our mistrust of public speech is a sensible response. And naturally, this mistrust has had an impact on poetic practice. It has destroyed an innocence we once had about the word—which has resulted, in turn, in a poetics of high style, irony, and gamesmanship.

◆

TO GET A taste of the way in which language itself moves ever more prominently into the foreground of poetic practice, compare the contemporary poem "Guidance Counseling," by Dean Young, to the poem by Smart and Plumly. Young's poem, which is a litany, playfully adopts the premise of being a kind of *Kama Sutra,* a sex manual:

Guidance Counseling

When the woman, her shoulders on the bed,
lifts her pelvis into the standing man,
it is called Dentist Office. When the man,
after an hour hiding in the closet, couples
with she of the silk flowered dress, snug
in the bodice, it is called Representational
Democracy. When the woman licks her burnt
finger, Tiny Garden Hose. Often as we grow
old, life becomes a page obscured with
too many words, like the sea with too many
flashes. Like my screaming may obscure
my love for you. How will we ever understand
each other? When the woman sits on the ladder
and the man churns like a lizard, stiff
in melting ice cream, it is called Many Dews. . . .

"Guidance Counseling" does not suffer quite the tone of existential unease in Plumly's poem, but here too Language, the

act of naming, preoccupies of the *foreground* of the poem's subject matter. Young's poem is not obviously about alienation, or
speechlessness, but tells a tale of comical disjointedness—Language is seen as a king of impediment between people. The poetic attention has been shifted from the realm of *nature* (perception) to the realm of *language,* naming. The poem could be said to
be celebratory, even erotic, in its playfulness—but it emphasizes
the nutty arbitrariness of the act of naming: *Tiny Garden Hose,
Representational Democracy, Dentist Office.* If we listen closely, we
can further recognize that these coinages are a parody, an echo,
of commercial product brand names, such as might be used to
name perfumes, sell ice cream flavors, or catalogue paint chips.

Young's poem, like Whitman's catalogues, enumerates the
cornucopia of phenomena—it playfully suggests there is a rich
universe of experience to be named, but in Young's poem, the
wonder is located in not in nature but in the stylistic dexterity
of artifice.

The Disconnect Goes Farther

The disconnect between words and things can grow much
more extreme, as can the emphasis on language as the preemi-
nent subject matter of poetry. For example, consider the following
1990s poem by a New York School poet, Jordan Davis. "Woman
(A.S.)" is a declarative litany, but what is being declared, or litan-
ized? Or is it the illusion of naming that is being demolished?

> The red moon is a banjo
> A jinx is a flat rate
> I am a drop shot
> Arizona is the sunrise of a fuckoff
> Tonight is the uncompiled code of an iced coffee
> A dart is the jimmy of a limousine
> My homeland is the dogma of brimming
> Turpentine is the Paul McCartney of your letting me know
> My lever is tomorrow
> A starling is a skinny boy
> A drifter is a paragraph
> Dehydration was your joyride
> Pacman is a percentage

Spelling is diamonds
The grey grass is conformist
Her hat is Alaska . . .

Davis's poem is just one representative of a widespread radical shift in the poet's relationship to the word; and, as important, we could say, of a radical loss of faith in the veracity of naming. "A Woman (A.S.)" seems pointedly intent on "neutralizing" some of our most deeply held assumptions about poetic language—that words are signs for "pointing," for instance; that a poem is "about" something; that metaphor serves a function of equation; even that a poem is a message passing between two people. Nor is Davis's poem "additive," in any conventional way—it does not, as it progresses, acquire more meaning, deeper emotional significance, or more coherence. In this particular poem, all these conventional presumptions about a poem are discarded, and displaced by style, gamesmanship, and a lesson about postmodern language.

One response to such a poetic mode might be to call it cynical; to accuse Davis and his tribe of the deepest nihilism, terminal irony, or poetic anarchy. Yet not all the evidence supports such a reading. Davis's poem exhibits too much pleasure and gusto to be written off as cynically hip or disillusioned. It is as if, freed from obligations of representation, sense-making, narrative, and autobiography, the fields of play are infinitely open to indefinable adventure. In our postmodern era of deeply mistrusted speech, it is a paradoxical fact that this uninhibited sense of play is a common characteristic of the New Poetry. The alienation, angst, and unease of one generation becomes the liberating poetic license of the next.

Another Piece of Perspective

For the last forty years, American poetry has been largely antitechnical in its orientation. A prejudice against fancy rhetoric, elaborate prosody, and erudite allusion might even be said to be part of the American character. Certainly an ethic of plainspokenness has characterized most of our poetry since the midcentury. The poetic revolution of the fifties and sixties, for

the second time in the twentieth century, took American poetry from the hands of specialists—academics, professors—and
"democratized" poetry into free verse plain speech. In the sixties, a hundred manifestos were written about the primacy of
inspiration. The anthology *Naked Poetry* (1970), for instance, in
its introduction, makes poetry out to be an explicitly "spiritual"
enterprise, governed by personal and psychic necessity. Poetry
is not engineering, asserts the editor, Stephen Berg. Academic
training and formal rules are only of secondary importance.
Poetry is not a profession, but a shamanic calling. Poetic shape
is discovered "organically," from inside out, not imposed by
some cultural convention, like that of the villanelle and sonnet.
American poetry—and our national spirit in general—is nat-
uralistic, pragmatic, plainspoken, and often anti-intellectual.
Our national pride is still "We don't need no book-learning;"
we have a kind of contempt for erudition and artifice. Thus, in
the last fifty years especially, plain speech and forthrightness
(not to mention joyful vulgarity and bluntness) have been the
stylistic emblem of democracy in American poetry.

This bias against artifice accompanied the flourishing of
the plain style in American poetics, which has delivered most of
the great American poetry of the last forty or fifty years, from
Allen Ginsberg to Adrienne Rich, from Sharon Olds to Philip
Levine. The plain style most trusts language in its spare, forceful
incarnations. Like all aesthetics, the plain style made a bargain
with the poetry gods—in exchange for the powers of intimacy
and clarity, it would forswear the more specialized possibilities of
prosody and artifice.

The New Poetry, in contrast to the poetry of forty years
ago, is extremely engaged in technique; preoccupied with formal experiment, technique, and matters of style, it celebrates its
artifice. Another way of putting this is to say that it is big on
gamesmanship. It is not so obsessed with "capturing" anything,
or apprehending a "truth." It is process-, not product-oriented.
It is deeply interested in exploring representation as a subject in
itself. In that sense, it often seems that the New Poetry's main
subject is its own *meaning-making,* or the nature of *means;* or, we
could say, perspective itself.

This might be a moment to reiterate one of the epigraphs introducing this essay, a statement by critic Stephen Burt: "Epistemology and theories of language—*how we know what we know, how we say it*—have become as central to contemporary lyric as psychoanalysis in the late 50s, myth and politics in the late 60s." The New Poetry is not about politics or psychology, but about how we perceive, and how language affects that perception. Thus the physics of representation often holds the foreground of poems now.

A contemporary poem which elegantly and wittily embodies the preoccupation of the New Poetry with saying and the emphasis on perspective is the second section of Robert Hass's longer poem "My Mother's Nipples." It, too, is a litany, but its preoccupying subject is *how* things are said, not what.

The cosmopolitan's song on this subject:

Alors! les nipples de ma mère!

The romantic's song

What could be more fair
than les nipples de ma mère?

The utopian's song

I will freely share
les nipples de ma mère.

The philosopher's song

Here was always there
with les nipples de ma mère

The capitalist's song

Fifty cents a share

The saint's song

Lift your eyes in prayer

The misanthrope's song

I can scarcely bear

The melancholic's song

They were never there,
les nipples de ma mère.
They are not anywhere.

Here, in the middle of an autobiographical meditative poem about family and loss, is a litany of adroit *examples* of how different kinds of speakers might sing about their mothers' nipples. In its rhythms, its wit and patterning, the poem becomes a language game, a catalogue of styles like fabric samples. It is as much, perhaps more, about *manners* of speech, as about experience. Or, to extend more credit to the enterprise, the poem is about how perspective and style—that of the utopian versus the capitalist, for example—shape perception.

♦

HASS'S PASSAGE IS a lyric interlude in a more general meditation, but its medley of transformations is not so different from Wallace Stevens's "Thirteen Ways of Looking at a Blackbird." Hass's poem might be called "Thirteen Ways of Speaking of My Mother's Nipples." The field of fantasia is not experience, but speech (a very specialized kind of experience). Hass's poem "performs" the anthropological idea that language shapes perception, that cultural givens create variations in consciousness. Hass's poem plays a speech game; and, through managements of style, it implies content. "My Mother's Nipples" also is about how sophisticated we've become as readers—if a straightforward narrative is now considered obvious, and insufficiently subtle, an elliptical style-game like this one is challenging, a sport for the reader as well as the writer. Whereas before, careful readers might have explicated the psychosymbolic implications of, say, a barn owl in a poem, they now can savor the structuralist wit of diction shifts.

That the poem is "fun" makes Hass's poem consistent with the New Poetry. That this litany occurs in the work of an older poet, a senior poet, is only an indication of the pervasiveness of our changing, transforming aesthetics. Section 2 of "My Mother's Nipples" exhibits gamesmanship, ironic playfulness, linguistic self-consciousness, and is style-intensive—an emissary of the New Poetry.

◆

CAN A POEM engage some of these self-conscious, anti-nominative (anti-denotative?) conventions, and handle content at the same time, in a nonconventional but truly enlightening way? Can gamesmanship, and a preoccupation with means, combine itself with meaningful, purposeful ends? It's not clear how the new conventions will combine with the old, but some new poems demonstrate new territories of possibility.

One final, intriguing example of litany, and of the New Poetry's relationship to style, gamesmanship, and representation, is Thomas Sayers Ellis's poem "Or," a poem produced by a "system" of using words grouped around the syllable "or." Ellis's poem presents a radical strangeness: it is a stylistically, "technically" intensive poem—declarative, it doesn't use the personal pronoun, or even much grammar. Impersonal and challenging, ominous, "Or" is a broken text, as well as an example of a "procedural" poem. The conventions that it invents, however, serve to deliver content in a new way—its *way* of saying has all kinds of implications about *what* it says.

> Or,
> Or Oreo, or
> worse. Or ordinary.
> Or your choice
> of category
>   or
>   Color
>
> or any color
> other than Colored
> or Colored Only.
> Or "Of Color"
>
>   or
>   Other

or theory or discourse
or oral territory.
Oregon or Georgia
or Florida Zora

or
Opportunity

or born poor
or Corporate. Or Moor.
Or a Noir Orpheus
or Senghor

or
Diaspora

or a horrendous
and tore-up journey.
Or performance. Or allegory's armor
of ignorant comfort

or
Worship

or reform or a sore chorus.
Or Electoral Corruption
or important ports
of Yoruba or worry

or
Neighbor

or fear of . . .
of terror or border.
Or all organized
minorities.

Disjunctive? Yes, "Or" omits transitions. In fact, it has no
verbs, or as the poet-critic David Antin would say, it "omits
explicit syntactic relations." Which is to say it leaves syntactic
relations implicit. It offers no discernible narrative, no essayistic
argument. The jumble of the poem is held in place by the repeat-
ing syllable, as well as the frequent rhyme in the poem—these

are the prosodic cohering agents of the erratic, dented, irregular dance of the selection in the litany. For yes, the poem is a list. That list is not really a "progression," which is to say that its ingredients don't *escalate* except through repetition; they don't accrue a meaning that grows slowly in import and precision. Yet the poem has a powerful undertext of experience: the history and present of American racial estrangement.

In Ellis's poem, the energy and mystery characteristically generated by ellipsis creates a poem that is something like a riddle—enigmatic, terse, dark; the identity of the speaker is repressed—there is no pronoun, no verb of action—but the dark subject matter oozes through; we sense the context of the poem—racism—leaking through the fragment. Dickinson says that art is a house that tries to be haunted, and it is striking in this example how alternative aesthetic devices make that no less true; the poem is haunted by the subject of American race history. The indirectness of the poem, its enigmatic stance, its randomness of signals (the way "born poor" and "Moor," "Yoruba" and "Electoral Corruption" cast a kind of unevenly distributed net of inference) allow a kind of menace of subtext to loom behind the poem—a haunting. Here, not knowing the intent of the speaker, not having *intimacy* with the speaker, works because it implies a lot of possible speakers that readers can imagine.

Ellis's poem brings us to an important aesthetic crossroads: the intersection or interface between *representation, expression,* and *construction.* Ellis's poem is not "organic" in any conventional sense—it does not arise from a discernable story, its content does not seem to preexist its form. In fact, one of the sources of the poem's energy is that it does not exist entirely either for its means or for its ends. Rather, they are commingled in the invention of the poem. At moments we might say the poem is making its way forward on the improvisation of the linguistic game; at times it is more emphatically asserting the referential urgency of its buried subject matter.

◆

IN EACH OF these poems, the act of naming is central, but radical differences in poetic emphasis are visible, from the representational (paying homage to the cat Jeoffry), to the theatrical ingenuity of language (a *Kama Sutra* position called "Representational Democracy"), to the tactile wit of language unhinged from function ("A dart is the jimmy of a limousine"), to the veiled, scrambled code words of a suppressed social history ("of Yoruba"). In each of these poems the act of naming is positioned in greater or lesser tension with the agenda of sense-making, with the desire for meaning. That dynamic dialectic (between sense and song) has always been a part of poetry, but the New Poetry is informed by new tensions, new understandings (the instabilty of language), and new possibilities. It shows no preference for narration, description, or confessions of the autobiographical self. It seizes hold of a radical new plasticity in signification, and thus—as has been the case in other revolutions—poems of the New Poetry head off in dozens of distinct directions. However, these diverse New Poets share some fundamental characteristics—they have an instinct for gamesmanship; they are stylistically and technically intensive; their starting point is the indeterminacy, the innate *unanchoredness* of language (which can animate either affirmative or negative impulses). They *feel* the plasticity of language. They also feel an obligation to approach knowing in new, often oblique ways. They might be called Experimental or Avant-Garde poets, but these labels seem, in 2008, encumbered with baggage—it seems better that they simply be called poets of the New Poetry.

MAGGIE NELSON is the author of four books of nonfiction: *The Art of Cruelty: A Reckoning; Bluets; Women, The New York School, and Other True Abstractions* (winner of the Susanne M. Glasscock Award for Interdisciplinary Scholarship, and a Creative Capital/Andy Warhol Foundation Arts Writers Grant); and *The Red Parts* (named a Notable Book of the Year by the State of Michigan). She is also the author of several books of poetry, including *Jane: A Murder* (finalist, the PEN/Martha Albrand Award for the Art of the Memoir), *Something Bright, Then Holes; The Latest Winter;* and *Shiner.* Since 2005, Nelson has taught on the faculty of the School of Critical Studies at CalArts in Valencia, California. She lives in Los Angeles.

Nelson was a featured writer at the 2009 Ohio University Spring Literary Festival.

All That Is the Case

*Some Thoughts on Fact in Nonfiction
and Documentary Poetry*

MAGGIE NELSON

THERE ARE THREE ISSUES THAT
seem to come up time and time again in my recent writing life.
I call them *fact, form,* and *skin.* Here I want to say a few words
about the *fact* part of that triumvirate.

By "fact" I mean, variously, those bits of world and word
that derive from research, observation, and/or sensory perception. This last gets complicated if you choose to include what
Jonathan Edwards deemed our sixth sense, "the sense of the
heart"—that is, the spiritual sense Edwards deemed as empiri-
cally rooted as the five senses described by Locke. Or if you
choose to include that which can be apprehended by intuition,
in the Bergsonian sense of the word (Bergson called his method
of intuition the "true empiricism"). Or perhaps most important
is Wittgenstein's notion of fact, as laid out in the *Tractatus:* "1.
The world is all that is the case. 1.1. The world is the totality
of facts, not of things. 2. What is the case—a fact—is the existence of states of affairs." The fact that there is a chair here is a

conjunction of a series of states of affairs: that the chair is standing on the floor; that it is brown; that it is made out of wood; that I have eyes; that I have language; etc. Writing from "fact" means becoming a better vessel to apprehend these states of affairs in all their complexity, and learning how to get that down.

To be honest, I don't really know what else there is, save imagination, which—although the holy grail for many writers—has never been of particular interest or availability to me. This lack of interest may be a form of self-protection, a case of exaggerating a deficiency into a virtue. Or it may be plain old sanity-producing self-limitation in the face of an overwhelming void. I don't really think so, however. I think of it more as related to a radical trust, that the most seemingly immaterial forces are, in fact, material. "Spirit is matter reduced to an extreme thinness: O *so* thin!" wrote Emerson. In any event, I haven't yet tired of fact, in this expansive sense, as a homeland for writing.

There are some books that I consider primers on how one might handle fact in a simultaneously expansive and stringent way. One of these is Peter Handke's slim, devastating book about his mother's suicide, whose title has been translated into English as *A Sorrow Beyond Dreams*. Within 76 pressurized pages, Handke lets "facts"—that which is knowable, reportable—become the condition of possibility for the unknowable. Using a network of simple signs, such as disruptive capital letters, he also *weirds* fact, introducing a Brechtian alienation to his crushing, personal subject matter. He explains his project at the start as follows:

> I am writing the story of my mother, first of all because
> I think I know more about her and how she came to
> her death than any outside investigator who might,
> with the help of a religious, psychological, or sociologi-
> cal guide to the interpretation of dreams, arrive at a
> facile explanation of this interesting case of suicide; but
> second in my own interest, because having something
> to do brings me back to life; and lastly because, like an
> outside investigator, though in a different way, I would

like to represent this VOLUNTARY DEATH as an exemplary case.

Exemplary case of what? Who knows? The important word here is "case"—case as an instance, a body, a husk, a state of affairs, a set of contingencies. "The world is all that is the case." A case is also an enigma, which promises a disclosure, or a solution, that never properly comes. Or, if it does, it arrives as a single moment of congealment, before the tide of becoming overturns the boat, and flux (in Handke's case here, a speechless chaos) reigns again.

Whether I am writing something that could be termed "documentary poetics" or more straightforward nonfiction prose, my interest stays with "fact" over "truth"—two terms which often get treated as synonyms, but which have totally distinct valences, histories, and implications. I never disregard truth (truth as in honesty, not truth as in a universal, absolute, moral, or religious truth). Nor do I deny that there may exist "truths" which are somehow greater than the sum of sublunary facts, or that a piece of art may provide momentary access to them. I'm just saying I don't go out in pursuit of such a thing. I aim to plumb that which can be sounded, even if it's a fool's errand. At the moment—or at least in my last few books—I don't want to "do" anything to facts, save apprehend, collect, articulate, arrange, and rearrange them. (Of course, this can be quite a lot!)

In this I know I differ from some of my peers. Eileen Myles's *Cool forYou,* Claudia Rankine's *Don't Let Me Be Lonely,* and John D'Agata's *About a Mountain* are but three quick examples of fantastic recent works that may or may not treat the business of fact quite differently than I do here. In conversation with these writers, I've sometimes found myself wondering if I'm more of a moralist, even if it horrifies me to say so. But even John Cage was forced to admit that, at least in a sense, he "could be likened to a fundamentalist Protestant preacher." Then again, being likened to something does not mean being that something. "If we interpret the word 'like' as a metaphor, or propose a structural analogy of relations . . . , we understand nothing of becoming" (Deleuze/Guattari).

And so I happily put myself in the "no imagination" camp. No "images." I don't mean that literally, of course—there are metaphors, similes, etc. in my work, all of which do create images, as do metonymic or adjectival descriptions. But for me there's a crucial compositional difference between knocking yourself out to create images that you hope will be startling (à la surrealism) and trying to express something as it is, as you perceived it, which sometimes produces an image, sometimes not. As Robert Creeley once said, even his most abstract poems are trying to say something very specific, it just might not be "'I love you,' or 'I'm sick' or 'where's the bathroom?'"

So, what do you do when you hit one of fact's many aporias? What do you do when you want to know something, or articulate something, that you simply cannot know? My rule to date—which is, of course, subject to change—has been that when I hit a place like this, I have to make the not-knowing part of the fabric. I mean, if it's that important to the piece and you can't figure it out, then you should probably just incorporate the confusion, and trust that the universe is retaining this navel of not-knowing for a reason.

James Schuyler is a glorious and wry practitioner of this approach, as in the opening of his poem "February" (from *Freely Espousing*):

> A chimney, breathing a little smoke.
> The sun, I can't see
> making a bit of pink
> I can't quite see in the blue.
> The pink of five tulips
> at five p.m. on the day before March first.
> The green of the tulip stems and leaves
> like something I can't remember,
> finding a jack-in-the-pulpit
> a long time ago and far away.

He can't quite see, he can't quite remember—no matter! He says what he can see, the way that he can see and say it. And he doesn't fuss over the rest, he makes space for it, he lets it be. "It's the yellow dust inside the tulips. / It's the shape of a tulip. / It's the water in the drinking glass the tulips are in. / It's a day like any other." The poem is an autobiography of Schuyler's roving, intent focus, and of the states of affairs of that February day.

When I talk about sticking with fact—abiding by its terms—I don't mean to deny the fundamentally interpretive function of the mind, or the representative task of language. In some ways I am making a humdrum point about the pleasures of working with givens, broadly defined—about the generative pleasures of submitting oneself, no matter how creative or experimental the project at hand, to the constraints of fact. Janet Malcolm offers a terrific and memorable metaphor for this submission in her book, *The Journalist and the Murderer:*

> [T]he writer of fiction is entitled to more privileges. He is master of his own house and may do what he likes in it; he may even tear it down if he is so inclined. . . . But the writer of nonfiction is only a renter, who must abide by the conditions of the lease, which stipulates that he leave the house—and its name is Actuality—as he found it. He may bring in his own furniture and arrange it as he likes (the so-called New Journalism is about the arrangement of furniture), and he may play his radio quietly. But he must not disturb the house's fundamental structure or tamper with any of its architectural features.

I've always loved being a renter, a hotel dweller, a percher, a squatter. I like the idea of packing-out-whatever-you-packed-in much more than the idea of making an indelible mark, planting a flag. This complicates the consolation promised by so many, from Shakespeare to Keats, that whatever suffering we undergo in this lifetime will be mitigated, or redeemed, or in some other inscrutable way offset, by the lasting power of the word. But since this consolation never did very much for me, it's not a great loss. Lately I have come closer to seeing the virtues of this approach by reading Hannah Arendt, who argues that one of the primary functions of the polis—if it is to maintain a sphere of genuine politics—is to preserve the words and deeds of its citizens for future generations. But my interest and understanding of Arendt's notion is in its infancy—I've spent far more time to date enraptured by the ephemeral, Frank-O'Hara-scrawling-poems-on-wet-napkins approach to a writing life. (Then again, poems are not politics.)

I am turned on by the originality, the freedom, to be found in this perching, this itinerant inhabiting. And in the prospect of thinking through others, with others, across others. "Men are lived over again; the world is now as it was in ages past. There was none then but there hath been someone since that parallels him, and is, as it were, his revived self," wrote Sir Thomas Browne, over four hundred years ago. Anne Carson has made a brilliant streak across the sky making such uncommon parallels and connections, from Thucydides and Virginia Woolf to Celan and Simonides. Her work is a glorious reminder of how much novelty and invention can be found in connection, in reading relations, in rearranging, in intuition, in "fact," in research, in the sense of the heart.

But to get back to Malcolm's metaphor. So, say you have to leave the so-called house of Actuality as you found it. Lots of play, no heavy tampering. Heavy petting, yes. I like this idea. It feels related to Wittgenstein's famous pronouncement, "[Philosophy] leaves everything as it is." I like this notion of leaving everything as it is. I would like the world as it is to be good enough.

Because so often it doesn't seem good enough. And I'm not just talking about the big picture (i.e., the social, economic, and spiritual sufferings that attend patriarchy, capitalism, racism, imperialism, cycles of violence, general mean-spiritedness and samsaric preoccupation), but also the small picture—the daily wishing-things-were-otherwise, even if just a little—our wanting to turn up or down the heat, our fault-finding with those we love, our complaining that we spend too much time on e-mail without doing anything about it, our trudging through the mud with a breaking sack of groceries, a child's kicking a dog in order to smear his pain outside of himself. And so on.

In the end, I believe it is true that, as Pema Chödrön says, "there is no cure for hot and cold." Working with the constraints of fact has been, for me, a means of trafficking with this "no-cure"-ness. A means of surrendering to it. The contemporary Chinese poet Mo Fei has said: "Poetry has to do with a satisfaction with limited things, a paring down. It is the acceptance of a certain form of poverty. It is not endless construction." I like this asceticism, this surrender to the *condensery,* as Lorine Niedecker once termed her writing life.

This sounds like an austere process, one of compression, of distillation. Certainly it can be. But it doesn't have to be. Listen, for example, to Alice Notley, in the final lines of her poem "Lady Poverty," from *Mysteries of Small Houses:*

> Beginning in poverty as a baby there is nothing
> for one but another's food and warmth
> should there ever be more
> than a sort of leaning against and trust a food for
> another from out of one—that would be
> poverty—we're taught not to count on
> anyone, to be rich,
> youthful, empowered
> but now I seem to know that the name of a self is poverty
> that the pronoun I means such and that starting so
> poorly, I can live

This poverty is not opposed to generativity, to flow, to fullness.

Now, I am well aware that the idea of a generative constraint is not a novel one. (Surely someone out there is thinking, *Hello, have you ever heard of John Cage? Oulipo? The basic sonnet structure?*) But I'm not really talking about the creative possibilities that can stem from strictures or structures. I'm trying to get at the sense of abundance—bodily, ethically, aesthetically—that can be found in this "leaning against," as described so movingly in Notley's poem.

Sometimes this abundance arrives via sheer intensity, via bringing the fire of your focus to bear on an isolated "case" in the world. Some of the most exciting "fact-based" projects I can think of right now are products of unremitting obsessiveness—of a constrained focus married to joyous verbal excess. I'm thinking, for example, of Wayne Koestenbaum's forthcoming opus, *The Anatomy of Harpo,* which spends hundreds of pages offering close readings of film stills of Harpo Marx from Marx Brothers' movies—of Harpo's gestures, his outfits, his expressions, his *becoming.* The genius of the project lies in the lavish, unbelievably sustained verbal and intellectual attention that Koestenbaum manages to devote to his mute subject.

A project of related excitement is art critic T. J. Clark's recent "experiment in art writing," *The Sight of Death,* a dense, beautiful book which chronicles Clark's obsessive viewing and re-viewing of two Poussin paintings on display in 2000 at the Getty Museum in Los Angeles. Here is Clark, in his opening pages, describing the process of making the book:

> It was not until several weeks into my note-taking that it dawned on me that the diary entries might make a book. Reading over what I had written then, I realized that if the notes were interesting it was primarily as a record of looking taking place and changing through time. Of course, bound up with that was the assumption, the truth of which I hoped would be demonstrated by the notes, that certain pictures demand such looking and repay it. Coming to terms with them is slow work. But astonishing things happen if one gives oneself over to the process of seeing again and again: aspect after aspect of the picture seems to surface, what is salient and what incidental alter bewilderingly from day to day, the larger order of the depiction breaks up, recrystallizes, fragments again, persists like an afterimage. And slowly the question arises: What is it, fundamentally, I am returning to in this particular case? What is it I want to see again?

Indeed, what is it about "this particular case," like Handke's "exemplary case"? The answer may never come clear. What IS clear is that it may demand "giving oneself over to the process of seeing again and again"—of allowing a state of affairs, be it that of a chair in the room, the composition of a Poussin painting, Harpo beatific beside his harp, the vista from one's desk on a February day, or the details of a mother's life and death, to come together and fall apart, to "alter bewilderingly from day to day." Clark suggests above that it helps to choose a worthy object, one with a good chance of repaying our attention. But, of course, the world doesn't always provide such assurances. Better, I think, to take the advice that Thoreau gave himself in his 1851 *Journal:* "The question is not what you look at—but how you look & whether you see."

CARL DENNIS, winner of the 2002 Pulitzer Prize for Poetry, has received numerous additional awards, including a fellowship at the Rockefeller Study Center in Bellagio, Italy, a Guggenheim Fellowship, a National Endowment for the Arts Fellowship in Poetry, and the Ruth Lilly Poetry Prize. His books include *Practical Gods, Poetry as Persuasion, New and Selected Poems: 1974–2004,* and *Unknown Friends.*

Dennis was a featured writer at the 2004 Ohio University Spring Literary Festival.

A Poem of Character

CARL DENNIS

IN A COLLECTION OF ESSAYS
meant to celebrate a long-lived literary festival that has featured both poetry and fiction, it seems appropriate to offer some comments about a kind of poem that comes closest to fiction, one that makes its central concern the presenting of a character whose life is separate from that of the speaker. In earlier ages, when poetry was often narrative or dramatic, this approach was central. Today such a poem occupies a sparsely populated border region between the genres. In this regard, we are the heirs of those Romantic poets whose primary form was the first-person lyric or meditation. The reader today tends to approach a poem with the expectation of confronting not characters in action but the voice of the poet, the poet as a constructed personality, who is usually presented as speaking to us directly, without the mediation of mask or narrative. Such poetry may include other characters, but usually those characters do not displace the poet's position as center of interest. So, in a Romantic poem like Wordsworth's "Resolution and Independence," the old leech-gatherer is given respectful attention, but the focus of the poem is less on him than on the

way in which he alters the mood of the poet. And in a post-Romantic poem like Robert Lowell's "Alfred Corning Clark" the focus is less on writing an elegy that makes an argument for the significance of Clark's life as a whole than on defining the particular influence that Clark exerted as a fellow grade-school student on the young poet, how Clark helped him deal with his own separateness and solitude. Lowell's poem may be said to have a plot, but it is not the plot of a life, or of the poet's reading of that life, but the plot of the poet's growing identification with Clark in the course of the poem, the plot enacted before us as the speaker moves past the tawdry public figure to the boy, and past dry wit to intimate observation.

Of course the moment one asserts centrality of the poet's first-person presence in the typical post-Romantic poem, a crowd of exceptions come to mind, starting with the Romantics themselves. One thinks of Wordsworth's great narrative "Michael," where the focus is not on the teller but on the shepherd himself, on giving him heroic dignity and pathos. And one thinks of Keats's comments in his letters contrasting Wordsworth's "egotistical sublime" to what he calls the "poetical character" as represented most fully by Shakespeare, his statement that a poet's character "is the most unpoetical of anything in existence, because he has no identity . . . is continually informing and filling some other body." Perhaps if Keats had lived longer, we might know him now as much for his narrative and dramatic works as for his lyrics. And later in the century we can turn for some of the best English poems not only to the dramatic monologues of Browning but to those of Tennyson, like "Ulysses," "Tithonus," "Lucretius," and "Maud," which suggest Tennyson's need to supplement his lyric impulse by reaching out to inhabit voices different from his own. Perhaps his example suggests that some poets often do their best work when working against their dominant mode.

A good contemporary example of this kind of dialectic is Louise Glück's most recent book, *A Village Life*. Over her career Glück has shown herself to be a strong lyric poet with a distinct focus on the poet's attempts to give shape to the stresses of personal experience. Though she has often resorted to myth to enlarge her canvas, to suggest that the poet's experience is part of a shared pattern common to the culture as a whole, the power of her poems resides in their distinctive personal voice, in its substantiation in a characteristic tone, syntax, and rhythm. But in *A Village Life* she has chosen to subordinate the character of the poet to a group of inhabitants of the "village" referred to in the title. This shift is particularly emphatic because she has chosen deliberately to forgo dramatic occasions that might present a persona at a moment of trial or conflict. Instead she tends to focus on a moment of retrospection in which the central figure, typically elderly, looks out over the landscape of a life and tries to come to terms with apparent limitation. The poems are reflective rather than exclamatory, deliberately risking loss of intensity as they gain in breadth of perspective. Rather than try to judge the book as a whole, I want to focus here on one poem that I think is not only successful in itself but helps to throw light on the difference between the focus of character-centered poetry and the focus of fiction. Here is the poem:

Walking at Night

Now that she is old,
the young men don't approach her
so the nights are free,
the streets at dusk that were so dangerous
have become as safe as the meadow.

By midnight, the town's quiet.
Moonlight reflects off the stone walls;
on the pavement, you can hear the nervous sounds
of the men rushing home to their wives and mothers;
     this late,
the doors are locked, the windows darkened.

When they pass, they don't notice her.
She's like a dry blade of grass in a field of grasses.
So her eyes that used never to leave the ground
are free now to go where they like.

When she's tired of the streets, in good weather she
     walks

in the fields where the town ends.
Sometimes, in summer, she goes as far as the river.

The young people used to gather not far from here
but now the river's grown shallow from lack of rain,
so the bank's deserted—

There were picnics then.
The boys and girls eventually paired off;
after a while, they made their way into the woods
where it's always twilight—

The woods would be empty now—
the naked bodies have found other places to hide.

In the river, there's just enough water for the night sky
to make patterns against the gray stones. The moon's bright,
one stone among many others. And the wind rises;
it blows the small trees that grow at the river's edge.

When you look at a body you see a history.
Once that body isn't seen anymore,
the story it tried to tell gets lost—

On nights like this, she'll walk as far as the bridge
before she turns back.
Everything still smells of summer.
And her body begins to seem again the body she had as a
      young woman,
glistening under the light summer clothing.

The first thing here that strikes the reader of Glück's other
work is how fully the character of the woman occupies the
center of the poem. This is a poem in the third person, in which
the speaker refers to the central character as "she," but the poet
is not present in the poem, neither in the foreground nor in the
background, as a secondary character or as a commentator.
All the thoughts here are presented as the woman's as she tries
to define, on her night walk, her perspective on the life she is
living in the present. We are in fact so close to the speaker's
thoughts that we may wonder why the poet did not let the

woman speak for herself. Why not a poem in the first person that begins,

> Now that I am old,
> the young men don't approach me
> so the nights are free,
> the streets at dusk that were so dangerous
> have become as safe as the meadow.

One problem with this alternative is a certain ambiguity about whether the "I" here is the poet herself or a free-standing character. If we read the speaker as the poet, the poem is much diminished, because it loses the power that comes with reaching out beyond the self, and the speaker risks sounding by turns self-pitying and defensive. But if we read the speaker as a persona talking to herself, we may still feel a greater self-consciousness on the part of this speaker than we do in the third-person original. She seems turned toward us in an act of self-presentation rather than turned toward an objective viewing of her gains and losses in old age. We feel closer to the woman in the third-person original, as we look over her shoulder from a limited, third-person perspective, than we do when she faces us directly. We are being invited to make the effort with the poet to figure out how the woman sees the world, rather than being told by the woman how she regards her situation. This sense of entering unseen into the woman's thoughts is emphasized as the poem develops by our coming to appreciate the difference between the poet and the woman, the way in which the woman is bound up with the rhythms of a village life that the poet may not have lived, and the way in which the movement of her meditation is grounded in the physical features of the landscape she is moving through, progressing in thought as she progresses from woods to field, from field to woods and river. This is not the deeply associative plot that we might expect from a subjective, post-Romantic poet, but more a plot that fits someone comfortable with the objective limits set by her immediate world.

Because the third-person perspective here is so deliberately limited to the speaker's perspective, we have to figure out on our own, as we do with the dramatic monologue, what we are to think of the woman whose thoughts we are entering. In a novel we might have the reactions of others to guide us, or some small distance between the narrator and the central figure to allow room for indirect judgments. Still, her engaging readiness to accept her life rather than to complain about it makes her immediately attractive.

And this claim to be free of fear is substantiated by the action of the poem, by the woman's enacting before us a moonlit, midnight walk through the town, and by the witty contrast she draws between her independence and the nervous rushing of the men as they return home to "wives and mothers." On the other hand, if her statement of gain seemed too easy, we might not find it credible, and the poet is careful, when the contrast between her youth and her age is repeated in stanza three, to state the loss more emphatically. She is like a "dry blade of grass in a field of grasses," not merely unattractive but anonymous, unnoticed. This concession gives more weight to the more emphatic restatement of the gain, that she is free not merely to walk where she wishes but to look about her and respond to the world as she never did before.

The woman's freedom is not only evident in the time she chooses to walk but also in the breadth of the space she walks in, her moving in thought and fact from street to field, from field to river, a freedom that suggests she can reach past the mental limits of the town to a more spacious apprehension of her experience. Here the contrast with the young people who used to gather by the river is especially telling. Having used the river as a trysting place, they have abandoned it now that it has "grown shallow from lack of rain," as if their connection to it is superficial, their presence or absence being dependent on the weather. But the woman responds to the landscape aesthetically, finding beauty even in the diminished river before her, in its containing "just enough water" to reflect the stars and the moon. This deeper, fuller, more sensuous response to the river prepares us for the final and most radical contrast between loss and gain presented in the last two stanzas. Without a body that is present to others, she is not merely unnoticed but somehow deprived of a history that the body records, and hence less present to herself. But the awakening of a fuller response to the world allows her to feel connected through her senses to the body she possessed when she was young, and hence, for a moment at least, to dwell in summer and her summer being. The acknowledgment of privation leads in the course of her walk to genuine self-expansion.

To the extent that we think of the poem as about the character's growth, it is both like and unlike the growth of a character in fiction, like it in that we have a sequence of widening circles of consciousness, but unlike it because this sequence is not marked by a sequence of actions and incidents extending over a significant passage of time but rather by a sequence of thoughts that take place in the course of a single meditation. In this sense, the speaker seems to be more free than a character in a work of fiction, less the product of her experience than the shaper of its meaning. This distance from sequential time is emphasized by her viewing the walk she is taking here as one of many walks she is accustomed to take. We are with her at a specific moment at the end of summer, with the river mostly dried up and the moon and stars reflected in its narrow channel; but the poem is also about the many other nights when she goes walking, now in bad weather when she stops at the town end, now in good weather when she goes beyond. To the extent that this walk is typical, not unique, it seems part of the cyclical pattern of nature, rather than part of linear history. But because she is aware of the pattern, her repetitions don't bind her to the natural world the way the young are bound to it as they go through their mating rituals. The woman's sense of repeated pattern provides the prologue for her final vision, in which she shows herself free, as the young lovers are not, to enlarge the boundaries of the moment, to make it inclusive:

> On nights like this, she'll walk as far as the bridge
> before she turns back.
> Everything still smells of summer.
> And her body begins to seem again the body she had as
> a young woman,
> glistening under the light summer clothing.

Because she can view the walk as part of a cycle of walks, the passage implies, she is prepared to see the past not as something lost forever but as something that can be recaptured. As rare and visionary as this moment is, it will return on similar occasions. In a novel that extends over the passage of linear time, the chief temporal contrast is likely between youth and age. Here the contrast is between life as understood as a forward temporal flow and life understood as a constant return.

Besides her greater freedom from linear time, the speaker here seems freer from the web of social connections that usually define the characters of a novel. This is a character who does not seem occupied with friends, family, or associates. No deep relations are suggested in contrast to her failed relations in the moment to those who do not see her. In a novel such isolation is liable to be presented as a deficiency, a privation that requires explanation, if we are meant to identify with the heroine, if we are not to see her as emotionally withdrawn. So Catherine Sloper, Henry James's heroine in *Washington Square,* attains emotional depth and insight in the course of the novel in which she becomes increasingly isolated, but we are left feeling that her isolation is an undeserved misfortune, not a blessing in disguise, the result of the failure of her father, her relatives, and her friends to cherish her as she deserves. In a poem like the one before us, however, "isolation" is far too negative a term for the fullness of solitude that the woman embodies. Partly this difference has to do with assumptions built into the genre of the lyric poem, its tendency to focus on a moment of insight rather than on a span of life. We do not ask of a moment that it display all the aspects of a character. But it also results from this particular woman's honest concessions about the cost of being invisible, an honesty that allows us to accept more readily her emphasis on the gain. To the extent that this gain is embodied in the fullness of her response to the scene around her, we can place the poem in the context of the nature poem, as the story of someone who can find comfort in discovering beauty that is not accessible to those incapable of an openness to the world around them. At the end of the poem, when the woman makes contact with her own young body, she is not only bringing the past into the present, but expressing her independence by acting as her own audience. The moment cannot be shared, and cannot be validated by any observer. She alone is aware of the glistening. And this audience of one seems to be enough.

Though the woman regards herself as a sufficient audience, the reader of course is aware of one other crucial witness, the poet who has chosen to make this woman the heroine of the poem, to understand and appreciate her perspective. If the woman is solitary, that solitude seems to have drawn the poet to enter her consciousness, so that the reader is aware both of the woman's separateness and of the intimacy of the poet's engagement with her. As a result the poem feels tender and giving even though its heroine does not exhibit these qualities in any obvious way.

What is being dramatized is an effort to do justice to someone to whom the world has failed to do justice, and in this effort the poem shares one of the central concerns of Romantic fiction, though its heroine is not a rebel against the social order or a victim of social convention. She is rather someone who does not need society to be complete. In the course of the poem, in the thought of a single moment that stands for many such moments, one of the invisible people is made fully visible, as we gladly follow the poet's lead, making her identification with the woman our own.

RICK BASS is the author of twenty-five books of fiction and nonfiction, including, most recently, a novel, *Nashville Chrome*. He lives with his wife and daughters in northwestern Montana, where he has long been active working to help try to protect as wilderness the last roadless areas on the national forests there. He has taught fiction writing at the University of North Carolina–Wilmington, the University of Texas at Austin, and Beloit College. His stories and essays have appeared in the *Paris Review, Narrative Magazine,* the *Atlantic Monthly,* the *New Yorker,* and others. He is a board member of the Yaak Valley Forest Council.

Bass was a featured writer at the 2006 Ohio University Spring Literary Festival.

Good Fortune Befell Me

Notes on the Writer/Editor Relationship

RICK BASS

THE BEST ADVICE I CAN GIVE
to beginning writers is to read as much as you can. This is hardly
original advice, nor is the complementary counsel to write as
much as you can. Those two braids can take you far; can lead
to great growth on their own. But if you are fortunate enough
to encounter a good editor to help reflect and participate in that
reading-and-writing regimen, it can be a wonderful experience.

That doesn't really pass for advice—*find a good editor*—but
instead falls more into the luck category, I think. A good editor—by which I mean one who is good for *you,* which is to
say, one who believes in your work, inhabits it, and places high
demands upon it, and you—can inspirit those twin braids with
an electricity, a pulse, that brings added life to the whole
venture: not just to the writing (and the reading), but to the act
of being a writer.

I was lucky, right from the start, in this regard, when I
met Carol Houck Smith in Utah in 1986, attending my first

writer's conference. She would become my first New York editor, ultimately publishing my first book of fiction, a story collection, *The Watch*. I had saved up the $285 for nonresident admission to the conference, and drove out from Mississippi in my old bald-tired truck with my dogs and girlfriend. The conference was held at a posh Park City ski resort, and there was no way I could afford lodging there, or meals—I was just faking it, as I was also faking being a writer. I just showed up and jumped in. Elizabeth and I camped each night in the high Uinta Mountains beneath cold summer stars, got up early each morning and built a fire, made coffee and cooked bacon by the side of the frost-laced stream, then drove thirty miles to the ski town still smelling of wood smoke, and showered in the hotel's poolside restrooms. We kept the hounds chained beneath the shadiest tree on the ski resort's lawn, where they sat like twin statutes, motionless, well-behaved for once, as if stunned by such non-Mississippi opulence.

I went to all the readings, panels, and workshops, and inhaled the ideas, lectures, examples. At some point, maybe midweek, Carol came over and asked, *Are those your dogs? What are their names?*

Homer and Ann.

Why did you name them that, where are you from, I've been petting them, they're sweet hounds, how long have you been writing, what do you write about, your girlfriend is quite beautiful, did you know that, how did the two of you meet? You drove all the way out here?

And so passed twenty-five good years. It's hard to put a finger on such luck, but I sense somehow that my dogs were connected to it. I had rescued them from the side of the road, and, immediately thereafter, good fortune befell me. They attracted her attention, and then her heart. I got to follow them down that path.

◆

CAROL WAS ENAMORED with and admiring of, though not necessarily addicted to, youth. She saw and savored the brightness and wonder of it. So many of her writers were young. She was so deeply fond of all of them. That's her euphemism for love. When talking about one of her writers, she would take a deep breath—her eyes would sparkle—and, as if preparing to utter the emotional revelation of a lifetime, she would say, "I'm *deeply* fond of him," or, "I'm *deeply* fond of her." We knew what she meant.

She was exceptionally mature, a quick intelligent mind and a fierce sense of justice—almost brittle, almost childlike. Sometimes she would get tense about something—some injustice—but then the adult part of her, the wisdom and maturity—the compassionate understanding—would kick in, and she would relax again, would regain her worldly editor's perspective on humanity. She was a good person. Though I do not recall whether I ever heard her utter these exact words, I find myself imagining that in these situations she might suddenly release her tension with a shrug and a laugh and the observation that "Ah, well, it's just life."

I never heard her speak ill of anyone or anything. Sometimes she would purse her lips and say nothing, but I never saw her once bother to go down the low road. She just wanted things to get better, to always get better, and had interesting ideas about how to achieve this, and if my memory serves me correctly, she was right 100 percent of the time.

◆

SHE WAS DEFINITELY old-school. I've been fortunate to stumble onto so many of the dwindling dinosaurs of the old school, now long gone. Harry Foster, George Plimpton, Carol Smith, Sam Lawrence: they all loved a good story, and, it occurs to me only now, that, despite being Easterners (though Harry had grown up in Houston, before moving to Boston and then Maine), they all loved the West, and, despite their legendary commitments to literature, they understood and appreciated the dilemma and passions of Western writer-activists. I personally never received anything but support from editors like Carol, who, though their business was literature, approved of the commitment so many of their writers had for the land and communities where their writers lived.

For a lifelong New Yorker, Carol just flat loved the West. It energized her each time she came out, and she welcomed opportunities to attend conferences in the West, where she cast a hunter's eye for young writers, young Western short story writers, still formative but overflowing with energy and vitality, upon whom she could wreak her intelligence. She gave and gave, but it's nice to consider that somehow she also received.

◆

WHAT WOULD SHE want said about her? She would remind us that she loved dogs. She inhabited the lives of her writers fully, as do so many great editors—psychologist, psychiatrist, financial backer, etc.—and she took a mother's or grandmother's delight in the day to day trivia of not just her writers, but her writers' children, pets, and hobbies. It should go without saying that she was fiercely loyal and bristled wonderfully at unfair reviews. She was attached to this world, engaged with this world, and somehow she did not let the superior magnitude or speed of her intelligence interfere in her relationships with those whose intellect and vitality was somewhat lesser; which is to say, almost everyone. This seems to me to be one of the many definitions or examples of grace, and of elegance.

She had the biggest, brightest, most inquisitive eyes you ever saw. The obituaries will describe her as being—as having been—birdlike, and that's fair enough. But like no bird I ever saw.

◆

IT IS AN axiom that no one ever has etched on his or her headstone, "I wish I had spent more time at the office," but damn, I wish I could do one more story with her, wish I had done one more story with her. She took delight in it, made it fun, she nurtured an intoxicating mix of the fun and the significant, the powerful, the enduring. She understood the failings of humanity and yet loved people anyway—all the more so, I think, for that understanding.

I can't believe I'm saying this. Particularly in my youth, I took so many hikes, canoed so many rivers, climbed so many mountains, went on so many hunts and camping trips. But in the case of Carol, my great friend and editor, I'll say it, just this once, and never again: Damn, I wish I could have one more day at the office.

MARY RUEFLE is the author of several volumes
of poetry, including *A Little White Shadow,*
Among the Musk Ox People, Apparition Hill,
Post Meridian, and *The Adamant,* winner of the
1988 Iowa Poetry Prize. She is the recipient of
both a National Endowment for the Arts and
a Guggenheim fellowship as well as both an
American Academy of Arts and Letters Award
in Literature and a Whiting Foundation Writer's
Award. She lives in Vermont, where she is a
professor in Vermont College's MFA program.

Ruefle was a featured writer at the 2010 Ohio
University Spring Literary Festival.

Someone Reading a Book Is a Sign of Order in the World

MARY RUEFLE

WHEN I WAS TWENTY-FIVE I began to keep a monthly list of the books I had read. Over time it became obvious that although some months I didn't read at all, and other months I read eight or nine books, on the average I read five books a month, or sixty books a year. Assuming this was more or less true from the time I was ten and began to read regularly—I know that in high school I was required to read a book a week and in college even more—I can calculate that I probably have read 2,400 books in my life, which may well be more than the average person, but in light of all the books there actually are, or in light of even another fact—that in the year 2000 200,000 books were published—it is a raindrop (though a very human one). Out of those 2,400 books I probably remember 200, or 8 percent. If asked to list them, I might not even get that far. What I want to know is: Is all this proportional, or does it reach some point where it no longer is? In other words, if someone has read sixty books in his life, can he remember them all, or only five of them? And is there anyone out there who has read only six books and forgotten them all? Doesn't that seem unlikely? Am I a super-fluous person because I have read more than I can possibly process, like an intake of food the body doesn't need, or am I a superfluous person because I have gone out and bought myself a new calculator?

◆

WHEN I WAS forty-five years old, I woke up on an ordinary day, neither sunny nor overcast, in the middle of the year, and I could no longer read. It was at the beginning of one of those marvelous sentences that only Nabokov can write: "Mark felt a sort of delicious pity for the frankfurters ..." In my vain attempts I made out *felt hat, prey, the city of Frankfort.* But the words that existed so I might read them sailed away, and I was stranded on a quay while everything I loved was leaving. And then it was I who was leaving: a terror seized me and took me so high up in its talons that I was looking helplessly down on a tiny, unrecognizable city, a city I had loved and lived in but would never see again. I needed reading glasses, but before I knew that, I was far far away.

◆

THE BOOK I was reading I was rereading. Because some time before that terrible day I had reached a juncture in my reading life that is familiar to those who have been there: in the allotted time left to me on earth, should I read more and more new books, or should I cease with that vain consump-tion—vain because it is endless—and begin to reread those books which had given me the most intense pleasure in my past, books I had all but forgotten in their details, but loved in the shadows they cast over me, the moods created by the very thoughts of them? And there was curiosity, too, the curios-ity of revisiting and remeeting. Some gigantic memory might strike me as being rather small in the flesh, or the altogether unremembered might strike me dead at a glance. It is not like returning to places; we don't find ourselves, in the fourth chapter of *Madame Bovary,* searching for the bakery that is no longer there. Our curiosity is always self-directed: Have *I* changed? Do I still love the Makioka sister who has diarrhea on the train in the last sentence? *Is* that the last sentence? Was I too young when I read Proust?

◆

I READ PROUST when I was in my twenties. I rationed that novel by reading one volume a year. I had a friend whose father was a man of letters, and he had said that once you read Proust there was no reason to ever read again, you had reached the end of reading, and as I was young and respected him enormously, I was afraid to finish that book, my incessant and increasing love for it was all wrapped up in this grotesque fear that my inner life was coming to an end before it had even begun. Which was correct. That's the cookie, isn't it? As for the larger statement—that once you read Proust there is no reason to read again—I found that, like most things, it was both true and untrue.

◆

THERE IS THE old story of Somerset Maugham reading Proust while crossing the desert by camel and of how, to lighten his load, he tore out each page after reading both sides and let it fall behind him—one wants to say the wind was involved, but on most days there was no wind. With or without wind, who has had a more memorable reading experience, Somerset Maugham or the one who came after him, the one who found and read a page here, a page there, in some strange new order with stellar gaps? Is this not a truer experience of *In Search of Lost Time* than *Remembrance of Things Past*?

◆

POLLARD: TO CUT back a tree to its trunk so as to induce a dense growth of foliage at its head. But it also means a hornless animal of a usually horned kind.

◆

TO REREAD A book is to make a pollard of it.

◆

IS THERE A right time to read each book? A point of developing consciousness that corresponds with perfect ripeness to a particular poet or novel? And if that is the case, how many times in our lives did we make the match? I heard someone say, at a party, that D. H. Lawrence should be read in one's late teens and early twenties. As I was nearing thirty at the time, I made up my mind never to read him. And I never have. Connoisseurs of reading are very silly people. But as Thomas Merton said, one day you wake up and realize religion is ridiculous and that you will stick with it anyway. What love is ever any different?

◆

THERE WAS ONE book I read not only at the right age, but on the right afternoon, in the right place, at the right angle. I read *The Waves* on an island, on a plotless day, when I was twenty-two years old, sitting on a terrace from which I could see in the distance the ocean and the horizon where it met the sky and the changing light that played there as the sun climbed to its zenith and descended again while I thumbed the pages and my blood pressure washed up and down with the words. *The Waves* is not one of my favorite books. But my memory of reading it is one of my favorite memories. I was very silly when I was young. I have that to be thankful for.

◆

I WAS VERY serious when I was in high school. I must have been, for my two memorable reading experiences from that time are very serious indeed. Both of them took place, of all places, in the classroom. Some English periods we were assigned to simply sit and read silently. We were reading *The Return of the Native* (or was it *The Mayor of Casterbridge?),* our silent minds on different pages. I was not in the classroom, of course; I was in Wessex. And there came the inevitable Wessexian moment: a letter, *the* letter, *the one that would make everything ok,* in the act of being slipped under a closed door, got wedged under the carpet on the other side, where no one would see it. This was awful. What happened then I could not foresee: my arm threw the book as hard as I could across the quiet room. Mrs. Pacquette asked me to explain myself. All I could do was stammer that it was *awful, awful, awful.* She supposed I meant the book. I did not. I meant the thing that was going to happen in the book, because no one was going to read the letter. Therefore I was not going to read the book. In retrospect I see that even then I was engaged in the mirrored eroticism of this compulsive activity, reading. Hardy grew up to be one of my beloveds, as did Kafka, to whom it happened next. "The Burrow" was in one of our textbooks. As the class sat reading silently, the silence seemed different. I was infuriated by my inability to understand what was happening in the story. What was happening? Deep inside myself I could not believe that anyone else was actually reading. I was convinced that a mistake had been made, that the printing plates—for I pictured them as such—had gotten smashed and all mixed up. There was a mistake. Was I the only one who noticed? Hadn't the teachers bothered to read the story? Their secret was out! There was a very special kind of attention that only I was able to pay to the story—it was absurd. And then I had a moment of doubt. *Who wrote this?* Perhaps *he* was the mistake, and not the story. I sat in the silent classroom and I heard all kinds of things—I heard the non-ticking clock tick, and the sweat beginning to form on my body, and the window glass was about to break into pieces. The pencil sharpener on the wall was salivating. I flipped to the back of the book where there were brief paragraphs about each of the authors, who they were, where they came from, when they wrote. Yes, I was certain now, the mistake was not in the story, but in its author. There was a mistake in the man. There had to be a mistake in the man because I was told where and when he wrote but not *why*. And of all the stories in our book, this was the one that remained starved and unfed unless I learned *why* he wrote it at all. I decided to hate the author. I decided to hate the author because he made me feel as if all my life I had been waiting for something to happen, and it was happening and it was not going to happen. It was many years before I understood that this was the secret labyrinth of reading, and there was a secret tunnel connecting it to my life.

◆

I FIND NOTHING *in my life that I can't find more of in books. With the exception of walking on the beach, in the snowy woods, and swimming underwater.* That is one of the saddest journal entries I ever made when I was young.

◆

READING IS HAZARDOUS. Here is a true story that proves it: a Chinese student, having read *The Scarlet Letter*, saw an American in China wearing a high school letter jacket with the letter A on the front and said *I know what that means.*

◆

HAZARDOUS EVEN TO the initiated: recently I was reading the notebooks of the Greek poet George Seferis (1900–1971). I was also reading, for the first and last time in my life, my own private journals, which I began writing when I was sixteen and ceased to write when I was forty. As is my habit, I was copying selected passages from the Seferis into a notebook. Later that evening I began reading a journal I kept twenty years ago. In it, I was reading the notebooks of the poet George Seferis (1900–1971) and had copied into the journal by hand my favorite passage, which was identical with the passage I had copied earlier in the day, believing completely that I had never encountered it before: *But to say what you want to say you must create another language and nourish it for years & years with what you have loved, with what you have lost, and with what you will never find again.*

◆

ALTOGETHER, I THINK we ought to read only books that bite and sting us. If the book we are reading doesn't shake us awake like a blow to the skull, why bother reading it in the first place? So that it can make us happy, as you put it? Good God, we'd be just as happy if we had no books at all; books that make us happy we could, in a pinch, write ourselves. What we need are books that hit us like a most painful misfortune, like the death of someone we loved more than we love ourselves, that make us feel as though we had been banished to the woods, far away from any human presence, like a suicide. A book must be the ax for the frozen sea within us. That is what I believe.

—Kafka in a letter, 1904

◆

WHAT KIND OF book would that dazzling human animal Consuelo sit down to read after she had finished wiping the blood off her hands and hidden once more her machete in the piano?

—Stevens in a letter, 1948

◆

THERE WAS AN anthology, a fat Bantam paperback with a glossy white cover (like the White Album) and something like an abstracted dove embossed on it, called *Modern European Poetry,* and it was mine, my joy and my solace when I was in high school; whatever problems I had with Hardy and Kafka in the classroom vanished in the solitude of my bedroom, which I shared with Rilke, Lorca, Montale, Éluard, Ritsos—everybody was in that book, I didn't have another book I loved half so much, I must have read it a hundred times, and then I grew up, and went out into the world, and promptly lost it.

◆

ONCE THIS THOUGHT crossed my mind: every time an author dies, out of respect a word should also pass out of being. A word the author loved and used repeatedly in writing—that word should be theirs and die with them. Nabokov: *quiddity*. But who should decide? The one who passes or the one who is left bereft? And who is the real widow? It is language herself, and her decision is clear: she does not want one of her children to throw herself into the grave pit of an old man. Quiddity: the essence of a thing; also, a trifling point, a trivial, inessential thing.

◆

I'VE OFTEN THOUGHT in acting classes they should make the actors perform scenes in which they are simply reading. And I've wondered what subtle—or remarkable—differences there might be between the outward appearances of reading different books. Early Tolstoy versus late Tolstoy might be an advanced assignment . . . that kind of thing. Or would they all appear the same? The outward idleness, almost slumbering, that does nothing to convey the inner activity, whether it be reverie, shock, hilarity, confusion, or grief. We don't often watch people very closely when they read, though there are many famous paintings of women reading (none that I know of depicting men) in which a kind of quiet eroticism takes place, like that of nursing. Of course, it is we who are being nursed by the books, and then I think of the reader asleep, the open book on his chest.

◆

I DON'T KNOW what my face conveyed while I was reading *The Seven Pillars of Wisdom* by T. E. Lawrence. It takes place in the desert and I read it in front of a woodstove during a four-day blizzard. I suppose it is very odd that I single this book out instead of, say, Lautréamont's *Les Chants de Maldoror,* an equally violent, anguished book, but I do. I've always defended *Pillars* as an unspeakable achievement in literature and disorder. In blood and displacement and an English lost in sand. Read only the first chapter and you will have read the human fate, "the implanted crookedness of things." I am exaggerating, of course. Like a book.

◆

THERE IS A world, which poets cannot seem to enter. It is the world everybody else lives in. And the only thing poets seem to have in common is their yearning to enter this world.

◆

FOR YEARS I planned a theoretical course called "Footnotes." In it, the students would read a footnoted edition of a definitive text—I thought it might as well be *The Notebooks of Malte Laurids Brigge*—and proceed diligently to read every book mentioned in the footnotes (or the books by those authors mentioned) and in turn all those mentioned in the footnotes of the footnoted books, and so on and so on, stopping only when led back, by a footnote, to *The Notebooks of Malte Laurids Brigge.*

◆

THE BURROW HAS probably protected me in more ways than I thought or dared to think while I was inside it. This fancy used to have such a hold over me that sometimes I have been seized by the childish desire never to return to the burrow again, but to settle down somewhere close to the entrance, to pass my life watching the entrance, and gloat perpetually upon the reflection—and in that find my happiness—how steadfast a protection my burrow would be if I were inside it.

—Kafka, "The Burrow"

◆

I HAD RECENTLY one of the most astonishing experiences of my reading life. On page 248 in *The Rings of Saturn,* W. G. Sebald is recounting his interviews with one Thomas Abrams, an English farmer who has been working on a model of the temple of Jerusalem—you know, gluing little bits of wood together—for twenty years, including the painstaking research required for historical accuracy. There are ducks on the farm and at one point Abrams says to Sebald, "I have always kept ducks, even as a child, and the colors of their plumage, in particular the dark green and snow white, seemed to me the only possible answer to the questions that are on my mind." It is an odd thing to say, but Sebald's book is a long walk of oddities. I did not remember this passage in particular until later the same day when I was reading the dictionary, where I came upon the meanings of the word *speculum:* 1) an instrument inserted into a body passage for inspection 2) an ancient mirror 3) a medieval compendium of all knowledge 4) a drawing showing the relative position of all the planets and 5) a patch of color on the secondary wings of most ducks and some other birds. Did Sebald know that a compendium of all knowledge and the ducks' plumage were one and the same? Did Abrams? Or was I the only one for whom the duck passage made perfect, original sense? I sat in my chair, shocked. I am not a scholar, but for the imaginative reader there can be discoveries, connections between books, that explode the day and one's heart and the long years that have led to the moment. I am a writer, and the next step was inevitable: I used what had been revealed to me in my own writing.

◆

WE ARE ALL one question, and the best answer seems to be love—a connection between things. This arcane bit of knowledge is respoken every day into the ears of readers of great books, and also appears to perpetually slip under a carpet, utterly forgotten. In one sense, reading is a great waste of time. In another sense, it is a great extension of time, a way for one person to live a thousand and one lives in a single lifespan, to watch the great impersonal universe at work again and again, to watch the great personal psyche spar with it, to suffer affliction and weakness and injury, to die and watch those you love die, until the very dizziness of it all becomes a source of compassion for ourselves, and our language, which we alone created, and without which the letter that slipped under the door could never have been written, or, once in a thousand lives—is that too much to ask?—retrieved, and read. Did I mention supreme joy? That is why I read: I want everything to be ok. That's why I read when I was a lonely kid and that's why I read now that I'm a scared adult. It's a sincere desire, but a sincere desire always complicates things—the universe has a peculiar reaction to our sincere desires. Still, I believe the planet on the table, even when wounded and imperfect, fragmented and deprived, is worthy of being called whole. Our minds and the universe—what else is there? Margaret Mead described intellectuals as those who are bored when they don't have the chance to talk interestingly enough. Now a book will talk interestingly to you. George Steiner describes the intellectual as one who can't read without a pencil in her hand. One who wants to talk back to the book, not take notes but make them: one who might write, "The giraffe speaks!" in the margin. In our marginal existence, what else is there but this voice within us, this great weirdness we are always leaning forward to listen to?

◆

IN THE 2001 Kentucky Derby, which I watched live on television, Keats ran against Invisible Ink. There was no way I was going to miss this race. But I waited in vain for one of the sportscasters to mention that Keats was an English poet whose only surviving descendants must live in Kentucky, where his older brother had immigrated healthy and had children, and I waited in vain for someone to mention the poet's famous epitaph—*Here lies one whose name was writ in water*—and its curious connection to Invisible Ink. In all the network, that great kingdom of connection, what had been read or remembered? It was as sad as a horse's eye. Keats lost. Invisible Ink placed second, but had he been third, he would have showed.

◆

THE ONLY BUMPER sticker worth having: OBLOMOV FOR PRESIDENT.

◆

AGAINST THE GRAIN. Nightwood. The Dead. Notes from Underground. Fathers and Sons. Eureka. The Living.

The Marriage of Heaven and Hell. The Sun Also Rises. My Little Home. Venus in Transit. The Wings of the Dove. The Journal of an Understanding Heart. Wuthering Heights. One Hundred Years of Solitude. Tristes Tropiques. The Tale of Genji. Black Sun. Deep Ocean Organisms Which Live without Light. The Speeches of a Dictator. The Fundamentals of Farming. The Physics of Lift. A Complete History of Alchemy. Opera for Idiots. Letters from Elba. For Esmé—With Love and Squalor. The Walk. The Physiology of Drowning. Physicians' Desk Reference. Bleak House. The Gospel according to Thomas. A Biography of Someone You've Never Heard Of. Forest Management. Black Lamb and Grey Falcon. Travels in Desert Arabia. The Collected Works of Paul Valéry. A Book Written in a Language You Do Not Understand. Withdrawn. The Worst Journey in the World. The Greatest Story Ever Told. A Guide to Simple First Aid. The Art of Happiness.

Credits

Lee K. Abbott, "Thirteen Things about the Contemporary Short Story That Really Hack Me Off." Copyright © Lee K. Abbott.

Rick Bass, "Good Fortune Befell Me: Notes on the Writer/Editor Relationship." Copyright © Rick Bass.

Claire Bateman, "Some Questions about Questions." Copyright © Claire Bateman.

Charles Baxter, "Stillness," from *Burning Down the House: Essays on Fiction.* Copyright ©1997, 2008 by Charles Baxter. Reprinted with the permission of Graywolf Press, Saint Paul, Minnesota, http://www .graywolfpress.org.

Ron Carlson, "The Wrong Answer." Copyright © Ron Carlson.

Billy Collins, "The Myth of Craft: Thoughts on the Writing of Poetry," originally appeared in an earlier version as "Craft Talk" in *The Southampton Review* Vol II, No 1 (Summer 2008). Copyright © Billy Collins.

Peter Ho Davies, "Only Collect: Something about the Short Story Collection." Copyright © Peter Ho Davies.

Jordan Davis, "Woman (A.S.)." Used by permission.

Carl Dennis, "A Poem of Character." Copyright © Carl Dennis.

Stephen Dunn, "Guardian Angel," from *New & Selected Poems: 1974–1994.* Copyright © 1989 by Stephen Dunn. Reprinted with the permission of W. W. Norton.

Stephen Dunn, "The Poem, Its Buried Subject, and the Revisionist Reader." Copyright © Stephen Dunn.

Thomas Sayers Ellis, "Or." Used by permission.

Louise Glück, "Walking at Night," from *A Village Life.* Copyright © 2009 by Louise Glück. Reprinted by permission of Farrar, Straus and Giroux, LLC.

Robert Hass, "My Mother's Nipples," from *Sun Under Wood.* Copyright © 1996 by Robert Hass. Reprinted with the permission of HarperCollins Publishers.

Robin Hemley, "Confessions of a Navel Gazer." Copyright © Robin Hemley.

Tony Hoagland, "Litany, Gamesmanship, and Representation: Charting the Old to the New Poetry." Copyright © Tony Hoagland.